Orayvi Revisited

Orayvi Revisited

Social Stratification in an "Egalitarian" Society

Jerrold E. Levy

with assistance from

Barbara Pepper

A School of American Research Resident Scholar Book

SCHOOL OF AMERICAN RESEARCH PRESS • SANTA FE • NEW MEXICO

School of American Research Press
Post Office Box 2188
Santa Fe, New Mexico 87504-2188

Director of Publications: Jane Kepp
Editor: Joan Kathryn O'Donnell
Designer: Deborah Flynn Post
Indexer: Andrew L. Christenson
Typographer: G&S Typesetters, Inc.
Printer: Edwards Brothers

Distributed by the University of Washington Press

Library of Congress Cataloging in Publication Data:
Levy, Jerrold E., 1930–
    Orayvi revisited : social stratification in an "egalitarian"
society / Jerrold E. Levy with assistance from Barbara Pepper.
        p.   cm.
    "A School of American Research resident scholar book."
    Includes bibliographical references (p.   ) and index.
    ISBN 0-933452-33-0 (HC : acid-free) : $35.00
    1. Hopi Indians—Social conditions.   2. Hopi Indians—
History.   3. Hopi Indians—Cultural assimilation.   4. Social
structure—Arizona—Oraibi Pueblo.   5. Oraibi Pueblo
(Ariz.)—History.   6. Oraibi Pueblo (Ariz.)—Social conditions.
I. Pepper, Barbara, 1949–   . II. Title.
E99.H7L49   1992
979.1'35004974—dc20   92-557
                                                                CIP

Cover: Entrance to the kiva during the Hopi Snake dance, Orayvi
Pueblo, ca. 1900. Photographer unknown. Courtesy The
Huntington Library, San Marino, California. (Pierce 2022)

To The Memory of
Mischa Titiev and Fred Eggan

Contents

Illustrations

Tables

Preface

DURING THE YEARS I lived on the Navajo reservation, from 1959 through 1964 and again from 1966 through 1970, most of my research dealt with Navajo social pathologies and mental health problems. Almost inevitably, however, the search for comparative data drew my attention to the Pueblo Indians, especially the Hopis. The contrasts were many. Navajos, for example, had higher homicide and suicide rates than did the Hopis. The Hopis, who had always been presented in the anthropological literature as sober and disinclined to drunkenness, had much higher death rates from alcoholic cirrhosis than either the Navajos or the nation generally. This finding led me to consider what had been written about the Hopis, especially the debate over the prevalence of anxiety and repressed aggression.

At first glance, the Hopi patterns appeared to confirm the notion that the stresses of acculturation accounted for the deaths from alcoholism, suicide, and homicide, which were found most frequently in the off-reservation border towns and in the "progressive" villages of Polacca, Kiqötsmovi (New Orayvi), Tuba City, and the government settlement in Keams Canyon. Further investigation, however, revealed that deviant behavior arose in all the villages, but the "traditional" villages expelled the offenders, who later died away from the reservation or in the "progressive" villages (Levy, Kunitz, and Henderson 1987).

We found that the children of marriages between Hopis and non-Hopis, between Hopis and the Haano Tewas of First Mesa, and between Hopis from different mesas were at greater risk for alcoholism and suicide than were the children of Hopi parents from the same village or mesa. These marriages were breaches of the well-documented rule of village endogamy. The "traditional" villages, however, also generated deviance, despite all their marriages being endogamous. Kunitz, Henderson, and I hypothesized that a desire to preserve homogeneity, expressed by the rule of endogamy, might be extended within a village to the social stratum represented by clans owning ceremonies as opposed to those with no ceremonial status; that is, a high-status family would prefer to have its children marry into families of equal status. Using this crude measure of status, we found that the risk for social pathology was highest among the children of "cross-status" marriages in Hotvela and the Second Mesa villages. The number of cases, however, was small, and social stratification was not dealt with extensively in the literature on Hopi. Beyond the fact that some clans owned ceremonies while others did not, and that some clans owned land that had been traditionally assigned to them while others had no assigned lands, there was little in the literature to suggest that social stratification was an important element in the organization of this small and ostensibly egalitarian society.

It was not until sometime in the 1970s that I came across Mischa Titiev's field notes at the Museum of Northern Arizona in Flagstaff, a copy of which was given to me by Barton Wright. The household census Titiev had made in 1933–34 of the village of Orayvi as it had been in 1900 contained the names, clans, society membership, and marital histories of almost every individual living in the village at that time. With these data I felt that a reanalysis of Hopi social organization could be undertaken. It was not until 1986, however, that this matter could be pursued further.

With the aid of two small grants from the Social and Behavioral Sciences Research Institute of the University of Arizona and another from the university's small grants program, the Titiev census was transcribed and coded, and genealogies collected by Edward Kennard from 1932 to 1934 were added to the data. A resident scholar fellowship at the School of American Research funded by the National Endowment for the Humanities for the academic year 1988–89 gave me time to do the first analysis and write a draft of this book.

None of this could have been accomplished without the assistance of Barbara Pepper, who shouldered the onerous tasks of transcribing Titiev's handwriting, checking each and every name to make sure the identification and Hopi spelling were correct, and deciphering the names in the enumerators' schedules of the 1900 United States census of Orayvi as well as those in Kennard's genealogies. The work was time consuming and exacting, and without Barbara's attention to detail the accuracy of the analysis would have suffered.

Throughout I had encouragement, help, and advice from the late Fred Eggan, whose interest in the Hopi was unflagging over the years. It was through his good offices that I learned about and obtained copies of Kennard's genealogies. I am also grateful to Sheila Johansson for guiding me to the enumerators' schedules of the census of 1900 and for encouraging me to look for the demographic consequences of stratification. My colleague of many years, Stephen J. Kunitz, has also given much-needed guidance and advice concerning the presentation of the statistical analyses, for which I am grateful. Emory Sekaquaptewa, Mary Black, and Kenneth Hill of the Hopi Dictionary Project at the University of Arizona have given generously of their time in matters linguistic, especially in deciphering Hopi names.

The variability in the spelling of Hopi personal and place names is often a great source of confusion. Throughout, I have used the orthography of the Hopi Dictionary Project, in the hope that, in time, it will become standard. Although the Hopi Tribe, in the latest version of the Hopi constitution, has approved the spelling of Hopi village names, these are Anglicized forms and are not always used consistently. As they are probably more familiar to the reader, however, the tribal spellings are presented here along with the Hopi Dictionary spellings:

TRIBAL SPELLING	DICTIONARY SPELLING
Mishongnovi	Musangnuvi
Shipaulovi	Supawlovi
Shungopavi	Songoopavi

TRIBAL SPELLING	DICTIONARY SPELLING
Oraibi	Orayvi
Kykotsmovi	Kiqötsmovi
Bacavi	Paaqavi
Hotevilla	Hotvela
Moencopi	Munqapi
Walpi	Walpi
Sichomovi	Sitsom'ovi
Hano	Haano

In recent years, younger Hopis have expressed considerable interest in family genealogies. It is my hope that the census and genealogies can be formatted in a way that will make the construction of these genealogies a relatively simple matter. The materials will be stored with the Hopi Dictionary Project and, ultimately, with the tribe—thus providing a data base upon which further historical reconstruction can be built.

Orayvi Revisited

CHAPTER 1

Introduction

MUCH HAS BEEN WRITTEN about the Hopi Indians of the American Southwest. The persistence of their village life and ceremonial system has attracted the attention of a wide variety of observers. Despite the numerous publications describing Hopi life, however, and a general agreement about the outlines of Hopi society and culture, virtually every aspect of that life has provoked discussion and disagreement among anthropologists. One of the early and enduring debates concerned Hopi character and personality. More recently, questions have been raised about the accuracy of ethnologists' descriptions of Hopi social organization and about the reasons for the fissioning of the Third Mesa village of Orayvi early in the twentieth century.

It is possible, of course, that the more that is written about a people, the more controversy is generated, as scholars of different theoretical persuasions using a variety of research methods become involved in the research (Heider 1988). Alternatively, the data may not yet have been analyzed fully, and a more thorough examination may serve to resolve some of the issues. This book represents just such an attempt. By reanalyzing material gathered by earlier scholars, two questions are addressed: Was Hopi social organization lacking in integrative mechanisms such that it could be characterized as fragile? and, Was the Orayvi split brought about by acculturative or by environmental and demographic pressures?

Fred Eggan (1950:116) noted that "Hopi society, despite appearances, is not completely integrated"—that because there is no centralized political superstructure, the clans tend to "assert their position at the expense of the village." Moreover, according to Eggan (1966:124), "crises involving the possibilities of major change were handled through the development of factions, which might lead to village splitting and the establishment of new communities." Titiev (1944:69) described Hopi social organization in much the same terms: "Such a social system rests on unstable foundations, for the more firmly people adhere to clan lines, the weaker must be their village ties. . . . Theoretically, the Hopi towns are in constant potential danger of dividing into their component parts." Yet when Orayvi split in two, it was not along clan lines; and no other Hopi village fissioned despite the fact that all were facing similar pressures. In several publications Whiteley (1985, 1986, 1988) has disputed Eggan's and Titiev's characterization of Hopi social organization, contending that neither Hopi clans nor the lineages they comprised were corporate units in any sphere of Hopi life. This dispute over the nature of Hopi social organization raises fundamental questions: Is there some aspect of that organization which has not been investigated in sufficient detail that differences of interpretation can be resolved, or have the theoretical biases of the observers obscured the reality, as Whiteley contends.

There is also considerable disagreement among anthropologists over the causes for the Orayvi split of 1906. Bradfield (1971) has proposed that a long period of drought in conjunction with over-population were the most important variables. Parsons (1922), Clemmer (1978), and others attributed the factional dissention to acculturative pressures; some Orayvis adopting a hostile attitude toward the federal government's demand that Hopi children attend school, others a more compliant policy. Titiev and Eggan have accepted both sources of stress as contributing to the ultimate demise of the village, but they implicate the fragility of the society itself as the principal reason.

Several ethnographers have noted that Hopi society is stratified, but other than recognizing the existence of social inequality they have "by and large written about the Hopi as an apolitical, egalitarian society" (Whiteley 1988:64). The reasons for this neglect may be several. On the one hand, anthropologists have tended to the view that social classes arise as a consequence of the production of an economic surplus; those groups that control and manage the distribution of this surplus become an elite, a class of managers. Less technologically advanced societies were, almost by definition, egalitarian. On the other hand, neither Titiev nor Eggan was an evolutionist, and both were aware of the many community studies undertaken by American sociologists that investigated the presence of class in the United States—a society that preached equality and considered itself classless. One wonders if these ethnographers were blinded by the received wisdom of their discipline or if the data at hand were too incomplete to allow them to investigate the matter further.

The major contention of this book is that a restricted and tenuous resource base required that Hopi society structure itself on an inequitable distribution of land, and that Eggan and Titiev recognized this and accurately described the methods devised to "preserve the core" of the land-controlling descent groups by sloughing off the excess population in an orderly manner during times of scarcity. But if land and water resources were so restricted that they could not be distributed equitably, these same constraints demanded a high degree of cooperation and social integration. In effect, an internal contradiction was created that kept the society in a state of dynamic tension, a tension that intensified or eased as droughts alternated with wet periods.

An ideology was developed that stressed the importance of both commoners and ceremonialists. The authority of the ceremonialist was balanced by his responsibilities to his "people." Each individual was responsible for his own actions and, of course, cooperation and non-aggression were highly valued. In addition to ideology and values, however, two social mechanisms worked to promote social integration and lessen potential conflict. Numerous marriage restrictions precluded the possibility of alliances among a few ceremonialist families; and the ceremonial societies, although controlled by specified clans, opened their membership to everyone. Every individual was encouraged to participate in ceremonial life and was given the opportunity to do so in personally meaningful ways. Even the ceremonies performed by these societies were integrated into the annual ceremonial calendar by a sharing of symbols and cooperation among societies.

Opposing these integrative mechanisms was the system of land control. The fields used to grow corn, the staple crop, were of unequal quality. They were assigned to various clans, some of which controlled the best fields, others fields of medium quality, and still others poor lands or none at all. There was, then, a ranking of clans that was sanctified by myth and ceremonial position: the highest-ranking clans owned the most important ceremonies; the lowest-ranking held at most a single position in a ceremony or no ceremonial duties at all.

Clan ranking, however, was not sufficient to deal with the pressures resulting from inordinate population growth. Each clan was composed of a hierarchy of lineages. The most senior lineage controlled the clan's ceremony and had the authority to assign farm plots within the clan fields. This senior, or "prime," lineage was supported by closely related "alternate" lineages which could assume its responsibilities should the senior lineage die out. "Marginal" lineages were expendable in times of crisis (Eggan 1966:124–25). In consequence, a marginal lineage of a highly ranked clan could be in a more tenuous economic position than a prime lineage of a less highly ranked clan if the population of the highly ranked clan exceeded the carrying capacity of its allotted land.

These characteristics of the social system were described by Eggan and Titiev based on observations they made during the 1930s, by which time this system of landholding had ceased to exist. Their conclusions were stated as assertions, but not demonstrated except insofar as their data were reasonably consonant with their conclusions. Had more data and better methods of analysis been available, these generalizations could, in my opinion, have been demonstrated with more certainty.

THE DATA

The material presented in this book tests the views of Eggan and Titiev, using, in the main, data gathered by them—many of which have never been thoroughly analyzed or published in their entirety.

The Titiev Census

In the course of two visits in 1932 and 1933, Mischa Titiev made a census of Orayvi which is probably the most detailed and informative census of an American Indian population prior to the modern period.[1] The census lists over one thousand individuals, grouped by household, who were either living or recently deceased in 1900. For each individual there is information on clan affiliation, ceremonial society membership, ceremonial offices held, marriages, children, factional allegiance, and where the individual went at the time of the Orayvi split in 1906. The handwritten notes were transcribed and entered into a personal computer. A data base composed of all individuals 18 years of age and above was constructed from the census and used to facilitate statistical analysis.

No ages are provided by Titiev, although whether or not the individual had died before 1906 is noted. Marriages are generally listed in order of occurrence, but there is no way to know which marriages took place after 1906. The approximate ages of individuals provided by the federal census of 1900 were assigned to the individuals identified by Titiev. One consequence of this approach is that the adult population used for analysis here consists of 566 people over 18 years of age, alive or recently deceased in 1900, compared to 622 people used by Titiev in his computations. His data base included a large number of individuals who were under age 18 in 1900.

All households in the census were located on a map of the village made by Alexander M. Stephen around 1880 and updated to 1900 by Titiev.[2] The material was provided by a single informant, the village chief of Orayvi, and checked by one other informant of a different clan.

The Census of 1900

The enumerators' schedules of the 1900 United States census list almost every individual living in the Hopi villages by household. An estimated age is given for each individual, and the relationships among members of each household are noted. For women, the number of children ever born and the number surviving as of June 1900, the month the census was taken, are noted (U.S. Census of Population 1900). The adequacy of the census has been evaluated by Johansson and Preston (1978). The population count is remarkably close to that made by Titiev some thirty years later. Some of the males of the "Hostile" faction were not counted, although we know from several sources that they were alive at the time. All but two of the adult women in the census were found in the Titiev census. Titiev estimated a total population for Orayvi and Munqapi of 863 (Titiev 1944:52); the United States census counted 858. This is the one major source of information that was not available to Titiev.

Third Mesa Genealogies

During the summer of 1932, Edward Kennard (n.d.) collected genealogies of all the inhabitants of the Third Mesa villages. Both he and Titiev were, at the time, members of the field party in ethnology led by Leslie A. White and sponsored by the Laboratory of Anthropology, Santa Fe, New Mexico. The genealogies made it possible to identify the lineages—prime, alternate, or marginal—to which most individuals in Titiev's census belonged. Prime lineages were identified by Titiev's information concerning clan houses and ceremonial offices held. Kennard never analyzed or published this material. By themselves the genealogies tell us little, but integrated with Titiev's material they become an important part of the puzzle.

THE ANALYSIS AND ITS TABULAR PRESENTATION

One consequence of merging these data sets is that the number of individuals for whom there was sufficient information varies depending on the specific analysis undertaken. Although, for example, there was a total of 566 individuals 18 years of age or more alive or recently deceased in 1900, only 556 had been born in Orayvi. Because only marriages among Orayvis were analyzed, the total in the appropriate table does not agree with the total population of adults. Rather than enumerate the nature of the missing data for each table, table 1.1 is presented here as a guide to the great variability of the totals displayed in each table in the text.

TABLE 1.1

	Women	Men
Total including recently deceased by 1900	284	282
Orayvi born	280	276
Orayvi married to an Orayvi	273	264
Alive in 1900	197	219
Alive in 1906	159	186
Alive in 1900, fertility history known	197	
Lineage known	231	182
Lineage and lineage of spouse #1 known	144	142
Age, lineage, and lineage of spouse known	111	104

THE ARGUMENT

After a review of what is known of Hopi prehistory, a speculative reconstruction of the evolution of Hopi society is presented in chapter 2. Special attention is paid to the history of drought, epidemics, and population, and to the early evidence for factions and intervillage conflict. A general outline of Hopi society and culture as they have been described in the literature is then presented to orient the reader to what is to follow. One is impressed with the fact that far from being a stable, slow-changing society, Hopi seems to have been almost constantly in a state of change, adapting to an environment that seems eminently unsuitable for agriculture.

In chapter 3, "Social Stratification," I examine the Hopi agricultural system, the types of fields and their varying quality, and the system devised to control and distribute this resource. The results of a computer simulation of the system in effect on Second Mesa in 1928 show that household survival was not ensured either by sharing equitably among all households in the village or by each household going it alone. Instead, limited sharing among a few households appears to have provided the maximum chance of survival. On average, these few households would approximate the size of one or two lineages. Although the extent of sharing among the households within a lineage or lineage segment or among affinally related households is not known, this sharing is taken to be the source of the clan and lineage system of ranking which I propose underlies the fact that no system of total village integration was ever devised. The fields allotted to each clan are identified and ranked according to their quality, resulting in a hierarchy of clans based on the productivity of the fields each controls.

The various ceremonies and ceremonial offices each clan controls are examined next, and each clan is given a score based on its ceremonial responsibilities. A simple regression analysis shows an almost perfect correlation between the ceremonial scores and the quality of land controlled. The system of clan ranking by ceremonies is nothing more than a translation of economic reality into the realm of the sacred, serving to sanctify the exalted position of a limited number of clans. Finally, the demographic consequences of this inequitable distribution of land are examined. Lineage position is the crucial factor determining fertility and survival of children. Women of prime and alternate lineages from high-ranking clans have high fertility rates *but* poor survival rates of their children. Having survived childhood, however, members of prime and alternate lineages lived longer than those from marginal lineages. The importance of lineages is confirmed, but this is definitely not an elite in the most often used sense. It appears that the need for heirs pushed high-status women to produce more children, thus inadvertently displacing an older sibling from the breast too early and exposing it to infectious disease. This also accounts for the often observed fact that high-ranking clans were usually very small and in danger of extinction.

In chapter 4, I look at the institutions that promoted social integration. The village was almost entirely endogamous. The numerous marriage prescriptions and the differing goals of men and women in acquiring mates resulted in a system of marriage alliances which cut across rank and lineage position. Marriage was, as Eggan proposed, a strong integrating mechanism. The degree to which the factional schism increased the divorce rate and led to marriages with proscribed partners for political purposes is also discussed. The other integrating mechanism, that of the ceremonial societies which drew their membership from all ranks and clans, is also analyzed. Although the ceremonial system was integrated symbolically and ideologically, the societies were less of an integrating mechanism than has often been thought. The majority of members in each society were drawn from its controlling clan or from related clans within the phratry.

The final chapters of the book examine the disintegration of Orayvi in 1906. Chapter 5 outlines general theories of factioning among North American Indians and the explanations proffered for the Hopi split in the anthropological literature, and briefly reviews the major events leading to the split itself. Most often such divisions have been viewed as responses to acculturative stress. In the case of the Hopi, several authors have suggested that the social organization was fragile and broke down in the face of population pressures during a period of severe environmental stress. More recently, a Hopi explanation has been offered as worthy of equal consideration.

In chapter 6, the structural-environmental hypothesis is tested and confirmed. Lower-ranking clansmen joined the Hostiles in significant numbers. Where clans of high and middle rank were split, prime and alternate lineages remained loyal to the village chief while marginal lineages joined the disaffected. Lower-ranked clansmen tended to be Hostile regardless of lineage position. The composition of the factions suggests that the Orayvi split was nothing if not a revolt of the landless.

The rhetoric of opposition to the White man and how the Hopis explained the traumatic events of the split and the years leading up to it are examined in chapter 7, which attempts an interpretation of events and motivations in historical perspective. The deterioration of the land and the onslaught of smallpox epidemics took place during a period of "unorthodox" village leadership. The Hopi interpretations of these events involve the shaping of myths to account for the position taken by the opposition faction. The traditional style of Hopi diplomacy constrained the village leadership to adopt a conciliatory stance toward the Anglo-Americans, which was used by the opposition to gather support. How the traditional leadership responded to these attacks and how some of the leaders of the Hostile faction were also constrained to adopt a conciliatory attitude are examined. Each side sought to buttress its position by appeal to tradition rather than to contemporary argument. Myths were politicized and prophecies formulated. Those announced prior to the events were never fulfilled, while post-factum prophecies were constantly adjusted to take account of events. Ultimately, the generally accepted Hopi explanation conformed to the general structure of Hopi myth and construction of history.

In the final chapter, after recapitulating the argument, I attempt to reconcile discrepant views of Hopi social organization as well as to reconcile Hopi and anthropological interpretations.

In large part, this book is a restudy of Titiev's (1944) *Old Oraibi: A Study of the Indians of Third Mesa*. Like that ethnography, this is a community study suffering from several of the limitations of such works in general. Community studies have been faulted for their lack of quantitative data, which makes comparisons with other studies difficult at best. Where such data have been collected, a lack of definitional clarity also makes comparison difficult. According to Bell and Newby (1972:16–17),

> the weaknesses of the community study method can be easily listed: it all too frequently rests on the observations of a single person, the procedures of observation are not systematized, there is no guarantee that another investigator would produce similar results, and the values of the observer cannot be disentangled from his data. In short, there must be some question about the scientific validity of the community study method.

It is my hope that by using Titiev's data in a quantitative manner this restudy is comparable to his. It is also my belief that his and Eggan's definitions of such phenomena as households, lineages, clans, and phratries are sufficiently clear that what confusion still exists may be clarified with a minimum of effort. In another respect, however, the lack of controlled comparisons with other communities limits some of Titiev's generalizations. What, for example, does he mean by a lack of integration, or a "fragile" society? This is surely a matter of degree that can only be evaluated by comparison with a society or societies with differing social organizations but facing stresses similar in degree as well as in kind. I have attempted to cope with this problem by providing some limited comparisons with other Hopi villages that had the same social structure but did not fission.

Although not dealt with directly in this book, one dispute of long standing among anthropologists concerns the nature of the typical Hopi personality and the degree to which it may be characterized as anxiety

ridden. Concerned as the controversy is with characteristics of personality, it is remarkable that it relies entirely on inferences about personality traits and not on direct observation or testing of such traits. It is
also concerned with generalizations that depend for their validity on
comparisons with typical personalities in other societies. The discussion then may be dismissed as exemplifying only too well some of the
criticisms leveled at studies of single communities. Nevertheless, all
those who have entered into the debate appear to have come intuitively
to the conclusion that its resolution may be important for an understanding of the Hopi, and the student of the Hopi is constantly re-
minded of the issue. It may, in consequence, be proper to recapitulate
here the highlights of the controversy in the hope that the reader may
arrive at some reasonable judgment after a reconsideration of Hopi social adaptation.

Although the Hopis have generally been described in the anthropological literature as peaceful, sober, and cooperative, for a time there
was considerable disagreement about the existence of covert aggression and hostility, and the degree to which Hopis may be psychologi-
cally maladjusted. On the one hand, Laura Thompson and Alice Joseph
(1947) were of the opinion that most Hopis actually lived up to social
ideals and that their typical personality was gentle, cooperative, mod-
est, and tranquil. Not only was the society highly integrated, but values
and world view were consistent and harmonious. Dorothy Eggan (1943)
and Esther Goldfrank (1945), on the other hand, concluded that the
maintenance of such a highly integrated society was achieved at considerable psychic cost to the individual. These observers have described
Hopi personality as marked by covert aggression, tension, suspicion,
anxiety, hostility, and even competitive ambition.

These contrasting interpretations have been discussed by Bennett
(1946) and Redfield (1955:132–48), who agree that it is not the facts that
are at issue, but the different value orientations of the anthropologists:
the one group approving the moral unity of Hopi life, the other disap-
proving Hopi society's authoritarianism and repression. Both Bennett
and Redfield believe the issue demands more explicit recognition of in-
vestigators' values and personal preferences.

Without disputing the influence observers' values may have in
shaping the interpretation of the data, Aberle (1967:80) suggests that

Hopi society was capable of displaying both sets of features depending upon the degree of stress a given community was undergoing at the time it was observed. According to Aberle, these contrasting features are closely related to one another and the truth does not lie somewhere in between but rather in understanding how these two aspects are bound together. Aberle, it seems to me, is placing emphasis on the often observed discrepancy between ideal and actual behaviors, noting that during hard times it is more difficult to live up to the ideal than it is during good times. The traits that fall short of the ideal would appear to be the unavoidable consequences of life in a generally harsh environment.

Siegel (1955) also relates the inferred anxiety and repression to the stresses generated by the Hopis' precarious adaptation to a harsh environment. According to Siegel, Hopi survival necessitated the development of a high degree of cultural integration, strong ties of communal solidarity, and a conscious conformity to expected conduct. Hopi methods of socialization demanded conformity early in life and emphasized the need for conscious control of emotions. In addition to internal controls, the community also recognized the authority of the ceremonialists to interpret and regulate behavior. At the same time, however, there were few sanctioned outlets for the anxiety and hostility generated by this process of subordinating the individual to the needs of the group. In sum, Siegel believes that these less than ideal personality traits are a direct consequence of the adaptive cultural mechanisms necessary for survival. This is similar to Goldfrank's (1945:535) belief that these traits are the "price" paid by the individual for achieving the social ideal. "For the individual the gains of such adaptive behavior are measured in a high degree of emotional security, the losses by the comparatively high level of anxiety which he must sustain" (Siegel 1955:47). But Siegel goes further and concludes that the maintenance of relatively high anxiety levels is conscious and is itself an adaptive pattern.

The problem, of course, is the difficulty in determining whether these personality traits were ever characteristic of precontact Hopi society, whether the strains placed upon the Hopi during the nineteenth century were more or less severe than similar strains placed on other North American Indian groups, and whether the anxiety generated by such stresses was more or less than, or qualitatively different from, what is found among other Indian societies.

It is possible that the reader, after considering the effects of drought, high infant mortality, and factional dissention, may wish to conclude that something may be gained by speculating about psychological states. Equally likely is the conclusion that such debate should be confined to studies for which psychological data have been gathered.

A final question, posed by the discussion of Hopi interpretations of and reactions to the events of the latter half of the nineteenth century presented in chapter 7, concerns how the anthropologist is to deal with the emic, or "native," point of view. Postmodernists have criticized ethnographic accounts for presenting the "etic," or observer's, view to the exclusion of the emic. Whiteley's handling of this issue in his book *Deliberate Acts* asks the reader to accept the emic interpretation on a par with that of the social scientist without further examination. Indeed, this seems to be the conclusion of several anthropologists in recent years. In his study of the Navajo Nightway ceremonial, for example, Faris (1990:13) faults Clyde Kluckhohn for not transcending functionalism, never "abandoning rationalism," and continuing "to tell readers what Navajo beliefs really meant and what such beliefs really did." Kluckhohn, Faris maintains, "could not admit alternate belief systems on their own terms." Again, readers must decide either to accept their own cultural boundaries, which constrain them to attempt to understand the Hopi according to the criteria of social science (as Hopis must attempt to understand non-Hopis according to their own criteria), or to accept the Hopi view as an alternative reality to which, presumably, the social scientist may also subscribe.

CHAPTER 2

History and Society

READING ETHNOGRAPHIC ACCOUNTS of preindustrial societies gives one a picture of worlds frozen in time. Most descriptions of tribal societies attempt to reconstruct the way of life that existed immediately prior to contact with modern Western society, using the present tense as if that life were unaffected by anything except perhaps the Conquest itself. The "little communities," as Robert Redfield called them, are presented as homogeneous: "Activities and states of mind are much alike for all persons in corresponding age and sex positions; and the career of one generation repeats that of the preceding" (Redfield 1955:4). Yet we know that many of these societies have changed over time and were already affected by contacts with the modern world long before being studied by anthropologists.

Ethnographic accounts of the Hopis follow in this tradition, despite their having been written during the late nineteenth and early twentieth centuries—some three to four hundred years after the Hopis' first contacts with the Spaniards. The sense of timelessness is due in large part to the absence of written records. And inherently, of course, any description of a culture at a given period of time cannot take change fully into account. Nevertheless, what little we know of Hopi prehistory cautions us against accepting their culture as either static or homogeneous.

Prehistory

Hopi is a Shoshonean language which, in turn, is part of the large family of Uto-Aztecan languages. According to historical linguists, the proto-Shoshoneans separated from the parent Uto-Aztecan group in northwestern Mexico and moved northwest perhaps as long as 4,000 years ago. By 3,000 years ago they had settled in southeastern California and had begun to expand and fission (Jorgensen 1980:68). The ancestors of the Hopi separated from their Shoshonean congeners and began moving eastward between 3,000 and 2,500 years ago. This was about the same time the precursors of the Pima and Papago (Tohono O'odham), also speakers of Uto-Aztecan languages, were separating from their closest Sonoran kin and moving north into southern Arizona.

The Hopi speakers probably traveled along the Colorado River and into the Grand Canyon and neighboring areas, where they acquired maize agriculture. From the time of their entry into the Southwest, no later than 500 B.C., until contact with the Spaniards some two thousand years later, they have been known from the archaeological record and identified by archaeologists as the Western Anasazi, occupying an area that stretched from Chinle Wash (running parallel to U.S. Route 191) in the east to southern Nevada in the west, and from southern Utah as far south as the Little Colorado River.

Sometime between A.D. 1 and 500, after the Hopi arrived in the Southwest, some Shoshonean speakers divided into the Shoshone, Paviotso, and Ute languages, as they spread across the Great Basin and into the Rocky Mountains.[1] The Great Basin was the area most recently occupied by Uto-Aztecan speakers, and it is among these linguistic relatives of the Hopi that Eggan (1980) finds examples of what he believes early Hopi life may have been like.

By about A.D. 600, the peoples of the Western Anasazi were substantially committed to agriculture (Gumerman and Dean 1989). The Western Anasazi remained relatively isolated from other Southwestern groups and, prior to A.D. 1000, were still living in pithouse villages while the Eastern Anasazi of Mesa Verde and the Chaco already inhabited surface pueblos.

From about A.D. 1000 to 1150, the Western Anasazi lived in small settlements, seldom containing more than 20 rooms. This was a period of expansion marked by an increase in population and the development of local distinctions. There were many small sites all over Black Mesa but, on Black Mesa in any event, population leveled off and began to decline around 1100. Generally these sites were small, averaging 2.9 rooms and occupied by single extended families. Environmental conditions improved as water tables rose and rainfall increased appreciably.

After A.D. 1150, however, the environment began to deteriorate. Reliance on agriculture increased, population expansion ceased, and people withdrew from peripheral areas. The uplands—northern Black Mesa, Shonto Plateau, and so on—were virtually abandoned, and people congregated along lowland drainages and in locations where alluvial farmland and water were available. There were major population influxes in the southern, lower areas of Black Mesa, as well as in Laguna, Long House, and Klethla valleys. In consequence, there developed a discontinuous distribution of sites in which centers of dense population were separated by nearly empty areas. Water tables continued to fall and erosion increased between 1250 and 1300, and the Western Anasazi achieved an unprecedented degree of reliance on agriculture. Gathering diminished in importance as adverse conditions combined to reduce the productivity of natural plant communities; hunting also contributed less than it had in the preceding period. The availability of water became a heightened concern. Large sites, concentrated in a few restricted localities, continued trends begun in the previous period. There were, however, few of these sites, and the majority of settlements continued to be small, located next to farmable alluvial bottomland. In some areas there is also evidence of conflict among settlements, presumably due to competition for scarce farmlands (Haas and Creamer 1985).

Beginning about A.D. 1300, the region saw a precipitous drop in the water table, the onset of severe gully cutting, and a significant decrease in rainfall. The entire northern area of the Western Anasazi became unfit for human habitation, and people moved to the southern end of Black Mesa where the Hopi villages are located today and to a few sites along the Little Colorado River where surface water was still available. By 1450, flooding of the Little Colorado destroyed some villages and irrigation systems, forcing people to join the villages along the southern edge of Black Mesa until only the area occupied by the present-day Hopis was still livable. These villages were larger, and they depended on water from springs and seeps at the base of the mesa and from alluvial flooding of the major washes.

Throughout the prehistoric period we see two major developments shaping the evolution of Hopi society. The adoption of agriculture most probably led to a transition from bilateral to matrilineal descent and, in time, named unilineal descent groups, or clans, came into being.[2] Human settlements were generally small and scattered prior to A.D. 1300, and social organization was most likely very much like that developed by the Western Apaches after their settlement in the Southwest. With the period of abandonment and site aggregation, however, we find the development of the Hopi system as we know it from the ethnographic literature.

We may speculate that, prior to the adoption of agriculture, Hopi society was very much like that of the Hopis' linguistic congeners, the Shoshonean speakers of the Great Basin, who occupied an area very similar to that of the Western Anasazi. Subsistence centered around the gathering of wild seeds, roots, and piñon nuts. Most of the hunting involved small game, especially rabbits, although deer were also present. Both men and women were important in subsistence activities. It seems most likely that the ancestors of the Hopi, like the Great Basin Shoshoneans, lived at what Julian Steward (1955) has called "the family level" of sociocultural integration. Three to five families made up a winter village which, with the coming of spring, would disperse, as single or at most two related families left in search of food to keep them until summer. In the fall, groups of families could come together to harvest piñon nuts, after which followed a period of festival, dancing, visiting, and courting as long as the food supplies lasted, usually about a week. There was neither "tribe" nor "band." Descent was bilateral and the sexes were of equal status. Headmen had only temporary authority when numbers of families came together for ceremonies and the piñon harvest.

Women did most of the gathering, and residence after marriage was matrilocal until after the birth of the first child, when the couple was free to join other relatives. The preferred form of marriage involved brother-sister exchange or, alternatively, the marriage of several brothers to a set of sisters. In many areas sororal polygyny and fraternal poly-andry occurred. Thus, although the sibling group was central to the social structure, we see the importance of women in matrilocal resi-dence and fraternal polyandry. Generally, marriage was outside the range of known relatives, although in some regions cross-cousin mar-riage of various types was practiced, including what Steward called "pseudo-cross cousin marriage," in which a step-cross cousin rather than a genealogical relative was married (Eggan 1980:174–75).

The Central Shoshone, with an environment more favorable than that of the Southern Shoshone, developed a series of institutions to increase local integration. "Marriage shifted to a cross cousin type in which brother-sister exchange was continued in the next generation where possible, increasing the bonds within the communities while re-ducing ties with neighboring areas. . . . Sororal polygyny and fraternal polyandry became more important and occasionally a woman might have two husbands who were not brothers" (Eggan 1980:178). A pref-erence for marriage with the father's sister's daughter and a prohibition of marriage with the mother's brother's daughter, with a corresponding shift in the terms for the two sets of cross cousins developed among the Gosiute of western Utah (Eggan 1980:179). This is an incipient form of patrilateral cross-cousin marriage and, given a unilineal descent system, would be marriage into the father's clan. In sum, if the preagricultural Hopis, adapting to an environment much like that of the Great Basin Shoshoneans, developed similar marriage and residence patterns, they would have been primed to develop matrilineal descent coincident with the adoption of agriculture. Titiev (1938) felt that the instances of mar-riage into father's clan found among the Hopi reflected an earlier pat-tern of preferred patrilateral cross-cousin marriage.

Murdock (1965:59, 184–259) has noted the tendency for societies with matrilocal residence after marriage to develop matrilineal descent once the conditions promoting unilineal descent are present. Agricul-ture in an arid environment often provides such conditions: agricultural land is limited and, in order to avoid dividing fields among heirs to the point that a family can no longer survive, a rule of inheritance favoring some children at the expense of others evolves. Where women do the gathering and postnuptial residence is matrilocal, gathering areas may be "owned" by women. Among the Southern Shoshone, for example, the women owned the seed harvest and were responsible for the welfare of their husbands, children, and any parents who might camp with them during the winter (Eggan 1980:177–78). From matrilocal residence and women's control of gathering sites or seed harvests it is but a step to women's control of farmlands and the inheritance of these lands through the female line.

Early Apachean social organization was very much like that of the Great Basin Shoshoneans, except that matrilineal descent may have been present prior to the Apache's adoption of agriculture (Dyen and Aberle 1974). In the Southwest, the agricultural Western Apaches lived in small settlements (local groups) near farm sites for most of the year. The local group was the largest unit with a definite leader and important functions (Bellah 1952:82–107). Generally, two or three named clans were represented in each local group, which contained anywhere from two to ten matrifocal extended families, some comprising 10 to 30 households (Goodwin 1969:146–47). In each group one clan predominated, and the group was known by that clan whether or not it contained others of equal size. Farmlands of a group were spoken of as belonging to its dominant clan, although use rights were not confined to that clan. The head of the local group was also spoken of as the chief of its predominant clan.

When the population of a local group exceeded that of the carrying capacity of its farmland, several extended families left the area to start a new settlement. As groups hived off and multiplied, leap-frogging over neighboring settled areas, named clans were found all over the Western Apache area. Although members of a given clan were often widely distributed, however, there seem to have been places where each clan was the strongest.

Clan linkages occurred in a variety of ways. Among the White Mountain Apaches, four or five related clans were grouped into exogamous phratries. In other areas, the linkages were more in the nature of chains. Clan A, for example, might be related to clans B and C, but B and C might not be related to each other (Bellah 1952:84). Marriage to someone of one's own or a related clan was prohibited, but marriage into one's father's clan was preferred, as was the marriage of two people whose fathers were of the same clan (shared father's clan). Thus, bilateral cross-cousin marriage seems to have been replaced by a preference for patrilateral cross-cousin marriage which, as clans developed, was represented by a marriage to someone of the clan of a cross cousin rather than to a genealogically close first or second cousin.

If, as I believe is most probable, similar developments took place among the Western Anasazi, a tendency to local group endogamy would have developed as both the reliance on agriculture and group size increased. Successive marriage alliances among two or at most three clans sharing localized farm sites decreased internal competition for land. At the same time, however, cultural homogeneity would be found over fairly large areas due to population expansion and the hiving off of local groups. Relatedness among people of the same clans and phratries would provide the basis for intersettlement cooperation.

By A.D. 1300, abandonment of large areas of heretofore habitable land led to fewer but larger settlements and, depending on the locale, to competition for control of shrinking agricultural resources. The tendency to local endogamy would be increased, but larger village populations would have contained a greater number of clans. This in turn would require the development of mechanisms to integrate the previously autonomous local groups. Marriage prohibitions had to be developed to preclude the formation of "cliques" resulting from father's clan marriage in successive generations. With the contraction of the Western Anasazi into the southern Black Mesa area, the social system of the Hopi as we know it was probably complete. Villages with populations in the hundreds, each containing a large number of clans and phratries, would also need to develop integrative mechanisms beyond that of marriage regulation in order to maintain village harmony, especially during hard times. Presumably, the katsina cult was adopted by the Hopi about this time and was one of the integrating mechanisms (Griffith 1983). In addition, the power of religious specialists and the emphasis on fertility and rainmaking probably reached its most intense development at this time.

Looking ahead to our discussion of Hopi demography during the late nineteenth century, it is important to note here that environmental stress was persistent throughout the entire prehistoric period and not a more recent phenomenon resulting from postcontact conditions. In a review of paleoepidemiological data, Martin has characterized the health of the Anasazi peoples in the following manner:

There were major and persistent nutritional deficiencies resulting from a corn diet; crowded and unsanitary living conditions
enhanced the chances of picking up communicable diseases
such as gastroenteritis; dental problems including caries and
periodontal disease were a major concern; most adults had ar-
thritis and spinal degeneration from carrying heavy loads; para-
sites such as lice and helminths were common; and infant and
childhood mortality were high. With respect to trends over
time, a continuum of health problems suggests that there were
changes in the patterns with an increase in diseases associated
with large and aggregated populations. (Martin 1990:14–15)

Society and Culture

By the time of contact with the Spaniards in 1540, the Hopi were living in seven villages: Awat'ovi and Kawaika by Antelope Mesa, with
farms along Jeddito Wash; Walpi and Sikyatki by First Mesa, with fields
along Polacca and Wipho washes; Songoopavi and Musangnuvi at Second Mesa, with fields along tributaries to Wipho Wash; and Orayvi at
Third Mesa, with fields along Orayvi Wash (Spicer 1962:189) (fig. 1).
Each village was politically autonomous, although the history of each
mesa shows that villages were founded as "colonies" of the principal
village. Where such clusters developed, villages have been identified as
mother, daughter, and guard villages. Village endogamy was the rule,
although marriage to a person from another village on the same mesa
was permissible. Even in the twentieth century, between 88 and 90 percent of Hopi marriages were mesa endogamous (P. Beaglehole 1935;
Levy, Kunitz, and Henderson 1987:378–81; Lowie 1929).

Orayvi contained some 28 matrilineal clans grouped into nine exogamous phratries when Titiev conducted his work in the 1930s. A census made by Stephen in the late nineteenth century revealed that the
number and names of the clans had changed little over half a century.
The clan was a named matrilineal descent group linked by mythological
tradition to several other clans to constitute a phratry. There were, on
average, three clans to a phratry. The same pattern was found in the
other villages, although the composition of the phratries varied somewhat and not all clans were represented in all villages (Eggan 1950:

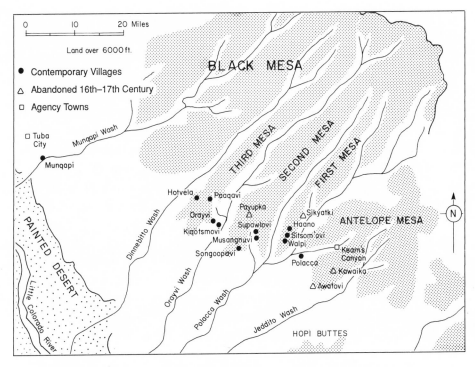

Figure 1. Black Mesa and the Hopi villages. (After Bradfield 1971; Brew 1979:514)

65–66). All told there were 12 phratries, 9 of which were present in Orayvi. Over 50 clans have been identified, although no village was home to all of them. There was considerable variation in the size of clans. At Orayvi in 1900, for example, the smallest clan contained only two individuals; the largest 61.

The best farmlands were located on the large alluvial plain at the mouth of the major wash. The next best lands were on the small alluvial fans on the many tributaries to the wash. Many farms were watered by the runoff at the base of the mesa cliffs, which seeped into the sand and provided sufficient moisture during wet years. Clans were, in theory, assigned fields by the Village chief, or *kikmongwi*. Some clans controlled excellent fields, others lands of lesser quality, while some few clans had no assigned lands at all. Clan-controlled fields were used to grow maize, the staple crop, although cotton was grown on these fields as well. The numerous plots used for beans and squash were owned by individuals, and there was no strict rule of inheritance governing them.

Orayvi set aside a number of fields of poor quality for the use of individuals who did not have access to clan lands either because their clan had no assigned lands or because its population exceeded the carrying capacity of its fields. Individuals were also free to seek suitable field plots at some distance from the village. Especially during periods of drought, this was a common practice. The clan, then, was not a group within which each member had equal access to land.

Depending on their size, clans contained one or more lineages. The "senior" woman of the clan was known as the clan mother. Her house was the repository of the ceremonial paraphernalia of the clan, and the authority to assign use rights to the clan lands was also hers. One or more of her brothers served as the priests of the ceremony controlled by the clan. One of her daughters, not infrequently the oldest, was chosen to succeed her as clan mother. The other daughters stood ready to take over the responsibilities of clan mother in the event the oldest daughter died. The lineage of the clan mother has been referred to as the prime lineage, those headed by her sisters as alternate lineages, and lineages more distantly related or having no known relationship as marginal (Eggan 1966:124–25; Connelly 1979:545–48). Marginal lineages were expendable during times of crisis. "In case of drought, all resources are concentrated for the preservation of the central clan core, and other clansmen may be forced to migrate or starve. As conditions improve, they may return and take up their former position and activities" (Eggan 1966:125).

The typical Hopi extended family was composed of a woman, her husband and unmarried children, and one or more of her married daughters with their husbands and children. As daughters' families grew and matured they would establish new households, so that at any given time nuclear families would account for between 40 and 50 percent of households in a village. Marriage was monogamous, and men went to live with their wives and farmed their fields for them. But men retained their ties with their natal households and were responsible for the discipline of their sisters' sons and the performance of the ritual responsibilities of their lineage. A woman, then, relied on her husband for economic support but on her brothers for ritual support.[3]

In Hopi theory the position of each clan in the village is determined by the order of its arrival and the ceremonial possessions it brought with it (Eggan 1966:125). The Bear clan is said to have arrived first in all the villages. Not only is the senior male of the clan the Village chief, or kikmongwi, but the clan also controls the major solstitial ceremony, the Soyal. And it is the Bear clan chief who controls the best land on the alluvial fan of the wash and who allocated land to the clans as they arrived.

Clan extinction was fairly common, and the Bear clan no longer exists on First Mesa. When a clan became so small it could no longer carry out its responsibilities, a related clan in the same phratry would take over and gradually assume the name of the dying clan. This process did not always proceed smoothly, however, as more than one clan might compete for the position. If the new clan was a worthy successor the ceremony would be successful, if not there would be drought or untoward deaths of the new priests. The events leading to the demise of the Bear clan at Walpi and the subsequent failure of its phratry mate, Spider clan, to successfully take over its position have been recounted by Eggan (1967).

Each ceremony was owned by a clan and performed by a ceremonial society, membership in which was open to individuals irrespective of clan affiliation, although the priests almost invariably came from the controlling clan. There were societies for women as well as for men. Women served as ceremonial "mothers" in the men's societies, and men served as priests and dispensers of medicines in the women's societies. All adolescent males were initiated into one of four tribal initiation societies, and the Maraw society was the equivalent of these for women. After the introduction of the katsina cult, boys and girls were initiated into one of the two katsina societies at around the age of puberty. Today, the men's tribal initiation societies are extinct and the katsina initiation has taken the place of the tribal initiation.[4]

What Titiev (1944:59) has called the "amorphous Hopi state" consisted of the village kikmongwi and six important chiefs who assisted him in the Soyal ceremony. This group convened annually after the conclusion of the Soyal to discuss matters of importance to the village and their interpretation according to the Hopi way of life. The Soyal chiefs were thought of as assistants to the kikmongwi and were the most prestigious of the ceremonial priests in the village. Their authority was religious, based on the supernatural power they controlled, and was neither legislative nor administrative. The kikmongwi could announce decisions, which were almost always given the weight of law, and the War chief wielded considerable authority during times of conflict. The others exerted formal authority only within their own clans.

Each of these officers was given a portion of Bear clan land to use as long as he held the office. In effect, a substantial economic benefit accrued to members of the "chiefs' talk," and the practice may be considered as an integrative device serving to reward the Soyal officers for their continued allegiance to the Bear clan chief.

In sum, the control of lands and ceremonies by clans and the weakness of an integrating village polity created a potential for divisiveness as the competing interests of clans often worked to disrupt village harmony. Despite the great prestige of the ceremonialists and the informal authority they exercised, there was no absolute power inherent in any single position or institution.

RELIGION, MYTH, AND HISTORY

The ceremonial cycle expresses two fundamental Hopi beliefs about the cosmos: the duality of existence, and the predetermined cyclical nature of time and events.[5] In Titiev's (1944:173) words, "there is a dual division of time and space between the upper world of the living and the lower world of the dead." While the sun is in the upper world, the lower world experiences night. Similarly, summer is the most active ceremonial season in the upper world. During this period, the lower world is performing ceremonies to help the living. Conversely, during winter in the upper world, ceremonies are performed which assist the dead of the lower world in their activities. Death in this world is nothing more than birth into the lower world. The duality of day and night, winter and summer, life and death, is repeated in endless cycles— oppositions interlocked in continuous rhythms.

The Hopi ceremonial year, synchronized with the agricultural cycle, symbolizes the duality of life and death. Winter starts at the time of the summer solstice (about June 22), when crops are growing and close to ripening. In July, the benevolent katsinas return to the underworld for the winter half of the year. Of the katsinas only Maasaw, the god of death and fire, walks in the world of the living during this period. Badger clan, whose tutelary spirit is the medicine animal, takes control of the katsinas during winter's dangerous months on Third Mesa. After the harvest, in October, the earth appears dead. The most dangerous period is reached in December (*kyaamuyaw*, the "dangerous moon"). Witches are thought to be especially active at this time, and people curtail their nighttime activities severely. This is the time to call the katsinas back to help purify the land. Soyalkatsina, as an old man still groggy from his long sleep, comes at the beginning of the dangerous month to prepare the way for the return of the katsinas. At the end of the month, the Soyal ceremony is performed, reaching its climax at the winter solstice (about December 22). The sun is enjoined to continue on its journey, bringing summer warmth to the upper world and thus ensuring continued life. All benevolent spirits are called upon to help purify the land so that humans may plant their crops safely.

During January, the katsinas respond to the Hopis' prayers and come to the villages in increasing numbers. But Badger clan cannot relinquish its guardianship until the land has been purified by the Powamuy ceremony in February. This month, *powamuyaw*, has been called "exorcising moon" (Parsons 1933:59) to emphasize the fact that dangerous and evil powers are removed at this time. But the word "purification" is preferable, as it includes both the idea of exorcism and that of making the earth whole again. The Powamuy ceremony accomplishes this by planting and germinating beans in the kivas: the first planting is thus conducted in the confines of sacred chambers. Once successful germination has taken place in the sacred arena, purification is completed and Badger clan relinquishes its responsibility for the katsina ceremonies to the Katsin clan for the next half year. From mid-April to mid-May nine sacred plantings of corn are made for the katsinas at several sacred places, after which the people may plant crops for themselves.

From the Powamuy in February until the Niman in July, the katsinas visit the villages and perform a series of dances. Starting in August and ending in October, the Snake, Flute, and women's ceremonies (Maraw, Oaqöl, and Lakon) take place. Tribal initiations are held once every four years in November. Although it occurs in the winter and is not an agricultural ceremony in the solstitial calendar, Hopis think of the tribal initiation as the beginning of the annual cycle. There are several reasons for this. The ceremony is initiated by a new fire ceremony, which is a rite of world renewal; Maasaw, the god of death and fire who welcomed mankind into the present world, appears; and the initiation is a birth into adulthood. The Wuwtsim and the Singers (Taw) are associated with fertility, the Agave (Kwan) with war and death, and the Horns (Al) with hunting. It is possible that the ceremonies of these societies contain elements of the older, preagricultural stratum of Hopi ritual and belief.

Predetermination and the cyclical nature of history are represented ceremonially during the Soyal ceremony, during which the complete sequence of events for the coming year is laid out. Each ritual, each dance, and the time for planting are magically enacted in advance, in the belief that these performances will determine the success of the coming ceremonies and ensure prosperity throughout the coming year. The Hopi word for magically predetermining such future events is *pasiwna*. Once this has been accomplished in the kiva, all that is devoutly hoped for must also happen at the appropriate time during the year that follows (Kennard 1972:469–70).

In the same way, the destiny of the Hopi was determined from the time of creation and is still being unfolded generation by generation. The myths of creation tell how life was created in an underworld and describe the events leading to the emergence into the present surface world. What happened in the underworld serves as the template for all that has happened since or will ever come to be. Hopi interpretation of contemporary events is, in consequence, a recognition of the repetition of past events in the present. The Hopi belief that future events will reflect this repetitive pattern is most often cast in the form of a prophecy.

The recurrent theme of dissention, flight from evil, and search for harmony is central to the emergence myths. Indeed, it is a key to understanding how the Hopi view their own society and how factions and dissention are explained in contemporary life. Life in the underworld became unbearable because of the activities of evil witches. Sexual licentiousness, lack of respect for elders and leaders, and indolence all contributed to a breakdown of the social order. The "chiefs" consulted among themselves and devised an escape into the world above the one they were in. Despite attempts to ensure that the witches remained behind, evil reappeared in the new world and the process started over again. This theme reappears in various forms in myths of clan migration detailing the destruction and abandonment of villages. Most often, the common people become dissolute and the village kikmongwi, in consultation with the other priests, must devise a way for them to be punished and for life to begin anew.

In the story of Palatkwapi, the kikmongwi uses supernatural power to destroy the village by flood. The survivors flee northward to join other Hopi villages near Black Mesa. Similarly, Pivanhonkapi is destroyed by fire, and the people are forced to flee into the wilderness to resume their wanderings until arriving finally at the Hopi villages. The destruction of Awat'ovi was planned by its kikmongwi, who arranged with the kikmongwis of Walpi and Orayvi for them to attack the village and destroy it. The story of Awat'ovi is based in historical fact; the factionalism resulting from the defection of some people to Catholicism was the manifestation of disharmony consequent upon the abandonment of the Hopi way.

Conflict between two villages may also lead to village abandonment in an effort to flee evil. Sikyatki fought with Walpi, Lamehvi with Qa'ötukwi, and Payupki with Tsukuvi.[6] It is not hard to see why Hopis experienced the factional dissention of Orayvi at the end of the nineteenth century as the repetition of a cycle of events, the outcome of which could be prophesied on the basis of knowledge of the past.

In general, then, it is the common people who forsake the Hopi way and the chiefs who arrange for them to be punished. No blame attaches to the leadership. Occasionally, however, a kikmongwi is blamed for a catastrophe. In a First Mesa story collected by Stephen in 1883, a kikmongwi "burned a bad fire" which made Cloud angry, and for three seasons nothing would grow (Stephen 1929:60–63). Factions are also occasionally described. A First Mesa version of the Horn clan migrations tells of a dispute over the choice of a new chief (Stephen 1929:67–70). The village was finally abandoned after the dissention led to fighting and killing, but after a new village was built yet another dispute over succession led to crop destruction and theft of fields. Similarly, following a dispute between the kikmongwi of Songoopavi and his brother, the latter left the village and founded Orayvi. Depending on the version, the blame for this episode may be laid at the feet of either brother (Courlander 1971:39).

Whiteley (1988:255–56) discusses Hopi *navoti*, a system of knowledge employed in explaining the past and predicting the future: "The nature and depth of understanding of *Hopinavoti* differs. *Sukavungsinom* [common people] are regarded as having a shallower understanding than *pavansinom* [ruling people]. . . . The structure of knowledge distribution in Hopi society . . . [may be] compared to established ecclesiastical structures differentiating a clerical hierarchy from a laity." In effect, the accepted explanations, the myths, and the prophecies are those of the pavansinom class. It is hardly surprising that the leaders are hardly ever to blame for the failure to live up to Hopi ideals, and that natural disasters are not the consequence of inept or evil leadership but are engineered by the pavansinom as a means to restore social harmony. The mythic explanations serve to preserve the status quo.

A number of myth traditions reflect the absorption of various populations over the course of time. Many tellings of the creation and emergence, for example, give Spider Grandmother and her grandsons, the Twin War Gods, the roles of creators. They help the people emerge from the underworld and make the present world habitable by drying the waters that cover it and killing the monsters that inhabit it. Another tradition, however, assigns the role of creation to two female deities (Huru'ingwuuti). Nor is there always agreement among the clan origin myths. Each clan has its own version of its wanderings prior to arriving in Hopi country. The order in which the clans arrived in a given village varies according to the clan telling the myth, as does the direction from which a clan came into Hopi country. For example, although Bear clan is generally conceded to have been the first to arrive in each of the Hopi villages, one clan myth puts Bow clan in Awat'ovi before Bear clan arrived in Hopi country (Courlander 1971:38).

In sum, the Hopi give the impression of a society striving for homogeneity and integration while constantly adapting to changing circumstances. The coming of the Spaniards and later the Anglo-Americans are but the most recent in a long series of events which the Hopis have had to fit into their view of human existence and its history.

CHAPTER 3

Social Stratification

THE HOPIS REGARD two social strata as significant in their lives: *pavansinom*, "most important people," and *sukavungsinom*, "grass-roots people" or commoners (Whiteley 1988:65). Pavansinom refers to those clans that control ceremonies and applies to all individuals of the clan, whether or not they are active participants in the ceremonial life. Thus, all members of the Bear clan are pavansinom even if they belong to marginal lineages and hold no ceremonial office.

The dividing line between the strata is not always clear, however. There is little consensus among Hopis about whether clans or the ceremonies they control can be ranked from most to least important or whether all clans owning any ceremony are pavansinom. Although all Hopis I have questioned on this matter agree that members of the clans that control the most important ceremonies are pavansinom, there is no consensus concerning the clans that own less important ceremonies, especially when the clan is a large one and many of its members belong to marginal lineages. Some Hopis believe that all ceremonies are important and the clans that control them are pavansinom. Others say that some ceremonies are more important than others—although there is little agreement on the ranking of the ceremonies—and that of the lesser-ranked clans only the prime lineages would qualify as pavansinom.

Although only two social ranks are formally recognized, certain statements suggest a more complex ranking. After noting that Hopis say it was "seldom that a commoner married into 'blue blood' families," Brandt quotes an informant: "If a middle class person marries into the chief's family, you have to live up to it" (Brandt 1954:25, 26). This suggests that three rather than two levels were recognized, and that more than ceremonial criteria were involved. While ceremonial position is a marker of rank, economic considerations are also mentioned:

> If a Hopi is asked to which class a given individual belongs, he will give a definite answer, depending upon the traditional tribal offices held by him or his family or his clan connections with persons holding such offices . . . The most fertile and best-watered sites near the village were in the hands of certain groups, while others had to be content with land of inferior productive capacity or with land away from the village, exposed to attacks from hostile tribes. The Hopi themselves say that some people were in the position of "slaves" and had to get their food by working on the land of other people. (Brandt 1954:23–24)

Economic differences are not only a phenomenon of the twentieth century. "Hopis say that in earliest times some families had much larger corn reserves than others," reports Brandt. To the question, Who are the high-class Hopi?, Hopis responded, "The people who have more things" (Brandt 1954:27–28).

The common view of the origins of social stratification as formulated by Engels (1942) holds that the ancient communism of primitive tribes was overcome when increasing technological progress led to a production of goods beyond the subsistence needs of producers, thus making some surplus available for market exchange. This development facilitated the specialization of both labor and money users, creating a new class of middlemen who could profit from purveying goods rather than producing them. Eventually the rise of a wealthy and powerful minority of entrepreneurs created a system of polarized economic classes. But an alternative offered by Fried (1960) has been found more consonant with many ethnographic data. Although societies could become stratified in other ways, Fried maintains that stratification was most likely to have arisen when population growth resulted in "differential access" to the wealth of nature by various kin groups, with some groups remaining in possession of the original richer lands (such as river bottomlands) and others becoming progressively poorer and more helpless in peripheral areas. This economic distinction could lead in turn to differential power and a political structure based on legal force. The questions addressed in this chapter concern the genesis of Hopi social stratification, whether these strata were based on differential access to key resources, the control and management of an economic surplus, or strictly on control of ceremonial office with no concomitant economic distinctions.

We have already noted that according to Hopi tradition the village of Orayvi was first settled by the Bear clan. The senior male of this clan is the Village chief, and the clan "owns" the Soyal ceremony which takes place at the time of the winter solstice. This is the premier agricultural ceremony, and it marks the beginning of summer and the agricultural cycle. As other groups came to settle in the village, the kikmongwi assigned them farmlands, in return for which they contributed a ceremony or some ceremonial function that benefited the village as a whole. The earliest arrivals received some of the best lands and also "owned" the most important ceremonies. The last arrivals received no land at all; nor were their contributions to the ceremonial cycle very great. If tradition reflects reality, the rank of any given clan ought to be based both on the quality of the land and on the ceremony it controlled. We will first examine clan landholdings to see if clans can be ranked according to the quality of their assigned lands. (It is not possible, at this late date, to determine accurately the *size* of clan holdings in 1900.) Second, we will consider the ceremonial status of the clans and the extent to which the land ranking corresponds to the ceremonial ranking. And finally, the possible consequences of an inequitable distribution of the land will be evaluated.

CLAN LAND HOLDINGS

Hopi corn requires a growing season of from 115 to 130 days, depending on when and where it is planted. The main corn crop is planted between mid-May and mid-June. The last killing frost usually occurs around mid-May, and the first frost of autumn at the end of September.

Corn is planted 10 to 12 inches from the surface, so germination is dependent on moisture from the snowmelt held in the subsoil and not on chance showers. Since summer rainfall comes in a series of thunderstorms occurring irregularly from place to place, fields that depend on local runoff are more drought prone than are fields watered by the flooding of washes that carry runoff from large areas of Black Mesa.[1]

Hopis make a distinction between *uuyi*, a plant, and *paasa*, a field. The former applies primarily to small patches of vegetables and early corn planted in the gullies at the mesa foot; the latter to the cornfields in general, but especially to those made where a watercourse, carrying runoff from higher ground, fans out on reaching the more nearly level ground of the valley floor. When speaking of clans controlling land, we are concerned with the cornfields (paasa), not with all arable lands (uuyi plots).[2]

Only two zones in the whole of the Orayvi valley are really suitable for agriculture: the fans found along tributary watercourses, *especially at their lower ends*; and the alluvial flats in the lower third of the valley over which the floodwaters of the main wash fanned out. Fields on the fans of tributary watercourses are *pisavasa*, or sand fields, referring to the thin layer of sand that covers them. They are better than the adjoining side valley slopes because of the volume of runoff that reaches them and because of the development of a special soil profile on the fans. The sand acts as a mulch to prevent evaporation, and the fertility of the loamy subsoil is renewed annually by the silt carried down in the floodwater.

Fields made on the old floodplain of the main wash were known as *nayavasa*, or "good fields." These were, by tradition, the best cornfields in the valley, and they lay in the 800 or so acres of alluvial flats below Orayvi where the floodwaters of the main wash spread out. Not only was the soil of this area quite different from the soil of the pisavasa, being a fine-textured clay where the other was a sandy loam, but it also lacked the covering of fine sand which acts as a mulch and reduces evaporation from the pisavasa fields made on the fans of tributary watercourses. Seeds planted on the alluvial plain were dependent on direct rainfall and on the floods that came down the main wash, *not* on the residual moisture held in the subsoil from the snowmelt of early spring. For this reason, and because of the greater risks of late frosts, the nayavasa were not planted until early June. This late planting was balanced by a shorter growing period due to a more assured water supply and to the greater heat of the main valley floor.

Both pisavasa and nayavasa had their fertility renewed annually by the silt carried down in the floodwater, but the fertility of the sand dune and side valley slope fields decreases until the field must be abandoned. It cannot be reclaimed until vegetable overgrowth decays and renews the soil after a few years.

For this study, Orayvi clan landholdings were located following Bradfield (1971:50) and Titiev (1944:62), and clan-owned lands were assigned a score according to their quality:

1. The highest score, 4, was given to lands on the upper half of the floodplain. "In the old days, the best land lay at the top of the old floodplain; the land at the very bottom only got water when there was a big rain up in the hills. The people used to dig banks and shallow ditches to spread the flood water; this had to be done each year, as the banks got washed away" (Bradfield 1971:51). In effect, the upper part of the floodplain that belonged to Bear clan was flooded every year even when the mesas themselves received little or no rain. The lower portion, although it may not have been directly flooded, could still be watered by digging ditches. The floodplain extended for about two miles downstream from the point where the wash debouched onto the plain. Just how far down the plain the waters would reach during dry years is not known, however; nor is the exact extent of the Bear clan lands, although Titiev's map shows Bear clan's holdings occupying the upper half of the plain. The wash received about 25 percent of the runoff from all of Black Mesa, so these fields received water every year regardless of drought conditions.
2. The fields of the lower half of the floodplain were assigned a score of 3 because ditches often had to be dug to get the water to them. It is not clear, however, that these fields were ever entirely without water, and for purposes of analysis these two best scores (3 and 4) are considered as one.
3. A score of 2 was given to fields on the alluvial fans of the tributary watercourses. Although these fields were renewed annually and

did not need to lie fallow, they only received local rainfall and so were more drought prone than the fields on the floodplain.

4. A score of 1 was assigned to fields along the upper reaches of the tributary watercourses without fans and to those directly on the side valley slopes or sand dunes. All of these were entirely dependent on local rainfall; they also had to lie fallow every few years.

5. Clans for which no assigned land could be identified were scored as 0.

6. A score of 1 was added to the scores of those clans whose prime lineages were given a plot of Bear clan land for their service in the Soyal ceremony (fig. 2; appendix A).[3]

There was a large tract of "free land" on which any individual, with the Village chief's consent, could lay out a farm. There were also many areas on the side valley slopes and upper reaches of tributary watercourses where small fields could be located. These fields provided land of the poorest quality to members of clans without traditional lands, and they served as a safety valve for clans whose populations had grown too large for the carrying capacity of the traditional lands.

Bradfield estimated that there was an annual requirement *for all purposes* of about 24 bushels of corn per person, 12 of which were for consumption and the rest for seed, storage, and barter. Two acres per person were required to yield this amount. In addition, the acreage planted for vegetables (beans, melons, and squash) required another .5 acres per person. A household of five to six persons would need about 12 acres to support itself, and a typical matrilineage is likely to have controlled some 40 to 60 acres (Bradfield 1971:22).[4]

Before burros came into extensive use during the latter half of the nineteenth century, the effective farmlands of the village came to approximately 1,800 acres in the lower third of the valley, with a carrying capacity of 720 individuals. According to Bradfield, fields had to lie within 4 to 4.5 miles of the village. Beyond this point, the time required to transport the dried cobs from field to village would have carried the harvest into November, when the first winter rains would spoil the crop. After burros were introduced, an additional 600 or so acres farther up the valley were cleared. The population expanded, in part through

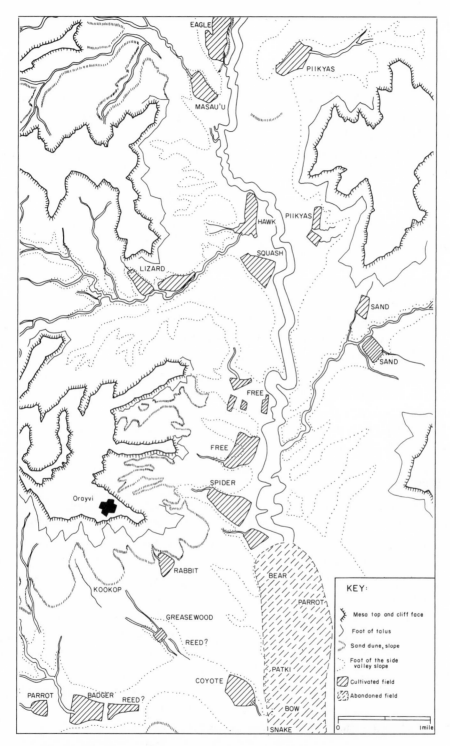

Figure 2. Orayvi clan lands. (After Bradfield 1971; Titiev 1944)

immigration, reaching between 860 and 900 by the end of the century. Whether or not the population of the village in 1900 exceeded the carrying capacity of the land will be discussed in the context of the Orayvi split; it is enough to say here that a total of 2,560 acres were being cultivated by the Orayvis at the turn of the century. Fields at an even greater distance, such as those at Munqapi and Paaqavi, are not included in the total. The acreage available at Orayvi would have accommodated a population of around 1,000 if all of it were used for food crops.

Five, possibly six, clans with a total population of about 100 people had fields on the floodplain. In addition, the prime lineages of another four clans (40–60 people?) were given plots of Bear clan land in return for their services in the Soyal ceremony. The 858 acres on the floodplain would have provided over 5 acres per person, twice the amount required for subsistence. The remaining 1,700 acres were farmed by 728 people with a per-person allotment of 2.33 acres—an amount barely sufficient for survival. There is no ethnographic evidence to suggest the existence of any formal mechanism by which families shared resources with unrelated families. In the memory of older Hopis, "every drop of water was precious, and there was never enough. . . . You never asked for a drink when visiting at a neighbor's house but went home to drink from your own water. . . . Every family was on its own. Even if a Chief had a lot of corn he would not share it" (Sekaquaptewa 1969: 21–22, 44).

Hegmon (1989) has modeled survival strategies for Hopi households and found that a system of restricted sharing among a small number of households (generally the size of a lineage) was consistently the best strategy, involving the lowest risk of failing to fulfill a household's needs for corn.[5] The restricted amount of gifting at naming ceremonies and various public ceremonies would not have been sufficient to serve as a redistributing mechanism. On the face of it, these land-rich clans and the prime lineages of the four clans receiving Bear clan allotments would seem to have had enough land on which to grow cotton and surplus crops for barter with the Navajos for sheep. The Hopis, however, view their classes of commoners and powerful people as based on ceremonial criteria and not on economic well-being, and the question arises whether the one is derived from the other.

CEREMONIAL STATUS OF CLANS

Many Hopis believe that "differing levels of importance attach to the ceremonies and the societies, although the ranking is not exact" (Whiteley 1988:59). Whiteley's scheme groups ceremonies into three ranks from most to least important as follows:

First-order societies
    Al, Kwan, Wuwtsim, Taw (tribal initiation societies); Soyal; Maraw
Second-order societies
    Blue Flute, Gray Flute, Snake, Antelope, Lakon, Oaqöl
Third-order societies
    Powamuy, Katsina

This ranking is based primarily on the sequence of initiations an individual could undertake. Because all children between the ages of 6 and 10 were initiated into the katsina cult, these were the most accessible and, presumably, the least powerful or important societies. They were, in consequence, of the lowest or third order. Young men could be initiated into one of the second-order societies without having to undergo tribal initiation. Similarly, Lakon and Oaqöl were open to all young women. They would be classed as second-order societies because tribal initiation was not a prerequisite. In order to participate in the Soyal, however, a man must have been initiated into one of the four tribal initiation societies and, as the Maraw was considered the female equivalent of the tribal initiation societies of the men, it and Soyal were considered most important and were classed by Whiteley as societies of the first order.

There are some difficulties with this scheme. First, as all males were initiated into one of the tribal initiation societies during the period we are examining, it is not clear whether participation in Soyal was based on initiation qualifications, individual choice, or some other considerations. Second, of the five women who held positions in the Soyal around 1900, only two were members of the Maraw society, suggesting that this was not a functional equivalent of the male initiation societies in any but the vaguest way. Some Hopis have suggested that Maraw was the oldest and, hence, the most prestigious of the women's societies.

The second problem concerns the importance of a ceremony in and of itself. While all Hopis see the Soyal as the preeminent agricultural ceremony, I have found none who view Powamuy as anything but indispensable, because it purifies the land. Here the tendency to strive for the integration of all the diverse pieces of Hopi culture into one "egalitarian" whole comes into play. Is it possible to see the rain-bringing function of the katsinas and of the societies responsible for their ceremonies as of lesser importance because these societies initiate all Hopis into the "secrets" of katsina impersonation? In like manner, may one relegate the second-order ceremonies to a lower rank because they take place during the winter and function to support the denizens of the lower world more than to help the living? To so conceive of them would be to drive a wedge, however slender, between the two worlds and hence to disrupt the unity of the dualism so important in Hopi cosmogony.

In order to avoid these and similar problems, I have adopted a scheme that does not differentiate among major ceremonies. Scores were assigned for major ceremonies; major political offices; ownership of a ceremonial kiva or of a common kiva; minor and extinct ceremonies; minor ceremonial offices; and impersonation of a Mongkatsina, or chief katsina (appendix B).[6] Scores were assigned in the following manner:

3 points. Ownership of a major ceremony. These ceremonies were always in the charge of a secret society.

2 points. (a) Ownership of a major political office. In addition to the Village chief, these were the five officers of the Soyal who assisted in this ceremony and held the "chiefs' talk"; (b) ownership of a ceremonial kiva.

1 point. (a) Ownership of a "common kiva"; (b) ownership of an extinct or "minor" ceremony; (c) right to impersonate a Mongkatsina; (d) ownership of a minor ceremonial office.

An ordinal measure of clan rank that could be assigned to individuals was devised, embracing both land and ceremonial scores. Initially, two ordinal scales were created. The first divided the population roughly into thirds; the second, far more restrictive, placed 15.4 percent of the population in the highest rank, 47.6 percent in the middle, and 37 percent in the lowest rank. The second and more restrictive scale matched the land and ceremonial scores the best. Table 3.1 displays the popula-

TABLE 3.1

CLAN CEREMONIAL AND LAND RANKING

Clan	Population	Land Rank	Ceremonial Score	Rank
Bear	19	4	7	3
Spider	31	3	14	3
Katsin	11	2	2	2
Parrot	31	3	10	3
Rabbit	61	2	2	2
Snake	6	3	5	2
Lizard	58	1	4	2
Sand	59	1	3	2
Reed	49	1	0	1
Greasewood	73	2	3	2
Bow	15	3	7	3
Maasaw	48	2	6	2
Kookop	22	1	1	1
Coyote	46	2	2	2
Water Coyote	57	0	0	1
Millet (*leehu*)	11	0	0	1
Badger	37	2	6	2
Gray Badger	33	0	0	1
Navajo Badger	11	0	0	1
Butterfly	5	0	0	1
Patki	36	4	7	3
Piikyas	45	1	0	1
Rabbitbrush (*sivap*)	3	0	0	1
Squash	9	2	1	1
Hawk	10	2	3	2
Crane	5	0	0	1
Sun	47	1	0	1
Eagle	21	1	1	1
Total	859			

Note: Population from Titiev (1944:52). I have omitted 2 Crows and 2 Cedars listed by Titiev but whom I did not find listed separately in his census. Clans are grouped by phratry.

tion, the rank of the land owned by the various clans grouped by phratry, the ceremonial score, and the ordinal scale of rank.

If control of agricultural resources determines ceremonial rank, the two scales should be distributed in much the same manner. This is in fact the case (fig. 3). A simple regression shows a strong positive correlation between the quality of the land controlled by a clan and its ceremonial score; that is, the better the land owned, the higher the ceremonial score. The probability that this could happen by chance is only 1 in 10,000.

If the land resource is distributed equitably among the members of a clan, we would expect to find that, on average, clans owning the best lands would be larger and those owning the worst would be smaller. This seems not to be the case, however. Clans owning the best (3 and 4) and the worst (0) land have significantly smaller populations than clans controlling poor and average (1, 2) land (table 3.2). At first glance, one might be tempted to assume that women of high-rank clans were

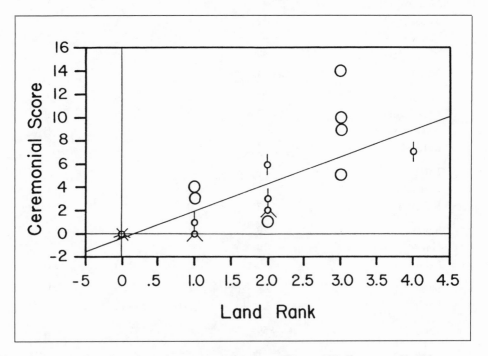

Figure 3. Land rank and ceremonial score. (R^2 = .627; F test = 43.683; p = .0001)

TABLE 3.2

CLAN POPULATIONS, LAND, AND CEREMONIAL RANK

	Population		Number of Clans	p^a
	Mean	Range		
Land Rank				
Good (3, 4)	23.0	6–36	6	<.01
Poor/medium (1, 2)	39.73	9–73	15	—
None (0)	17.86	3–57	7	<.01
Ceremonial Rank				
High	26.4	15–36	5	<.01
Middle	40.9	6–73	10	—
Low	24.46	3–57	13	<.01

Note: Population data are from Titiev's (1944) total clan populations, all ages. N = 859.
[a]Level of significance for the Mann-Whitney U Test. In each table the highest and lowest groups are compared to the middle group.

restricting the number of children born in an effort to preserve their resource advantage, while the lower-ranked clans were suffering higher mortality rates generally.

In respect of fertility, however, there were no significant differences in the average number of children born to women between the ages of 18 and 32. After age 33, though, women of prime and alternate lineages in high-ranking clans had significantly *more* children per bearing woman than all other women (table 3.3).[7] These women of the highest possible status not only bore more children (10 per woman over 33 years as compared to 7.5 for all other women in the same age cohort), but their children also had the poorest survival rates (28.6 percent versus 47.3 percent).[8] It would appear that, rather than controlling birth rates, the high-status women were trying to produce heirs and tended to shorten birth spacing, thus displacing the older sibling from the breast and inadvertently exposing it to a variety of infectious diseases.[9] In an effort to preserve their position, it seems that the prime lineages of the leading clans were engaging in a self-defeating practice.

TABLE 3.3

FERTILITY AND CHILDREN'S SURVIVAL RATES FOR WOMEN
33+ YEARS OF AGE, BY RANK AND LINEAGE

Rank	Lineage	N	Mean # Births	p^a	Mean # Survived	p^a	% Survived	p^a
High	P/A[b]	7	10	—	2.8	—	28.6	—
	Marg[c]	4	7.5		3.75		50.0	.04
Middle	P/A	16	8.1		5.0	<.01	53.8	.001
	Marg	22	7.6	.02	3.5		46.7	.06
Low	P/A	14	7.9		3.4		36.9	
	Marg	9	7.7		4.0		52.2	.05

[a] Level of significance for the Mann-Whitney U Test. Each group is compared to the high-rank, prime/alternate lineage women.
[b] P/A = Prime/alternate lineage.
[c] Marg = Marginal lineage.

Once having survived childhood, however, members of prime and alternate lineages enjoyed greater longevity than those of marginal lineages (table 3.4). A rule of primogeniture might acccount for the significant differences in age between members of marginal lineages and those of the senior lineages. If clan mothers consistently selected their eldest daughters to succeed them, there would have been a tendency for women of the prime lineages to have been older than their younger sisters who headed alternate lineages. In two generations, as the daughters of these younger sisters became heads of marginal lineages, there would have been a persisting tendency for members of marginal lineages to have been younger than members of either alternate or prime lineages.

This seems not to have been the case, however. Even the marginal lineages with no genealogical connection to the prime and alternate lineages were about as young as the members of marginal lineages descended from the women of alternate lineages. Moreover, men of prime lineages, who included all brothers of a clan mother regardless of age, were older than the men of marginal lineages by as many years as were their sisters than the women of marginal lineages.

The more plausible explanation of these age differences is that

TABLE 3.4

AGE OF ADULTS OVER 18 BY LINEAGE, AND AGE OF WOMEN BY LINEAGE AND LINEAGE OF HUSBAND

Lineage	Women			Men		
	N	Mean Age	p^a	N	Mean Age	p^a
Prime	29	37.7	—	53	40.9	—
Alternate	39	35.8	n.s.[b]			
Related Marg[c]	89	31.0	<.01	72	31.4	<.01
Unrelated Marg	14	32.1	.01	9	32.4	<.01

Woman's Lineage	Husband's Lineage	N	Mean Age	Range	p^a
P/A[d]	Prime	17	37.2	21–60	—
P/A	Marg	25	33.0	19–60	n.s.
Marg	Prime	24	34.5	19–60	n.s.
Marg	Marg	44	28.7	18–59	.002

[a]Level of significance for the Mann-Whitney U Test. The groups in the top half of the table are compared with the Prime lineage; those in the bottom half, with the P/A to Prime group.
[b]n.s. = Not significant.
[c]Marg = Marginal.
[d]P/A = Prime/alternate.

members of prime and alternate lineages controlled the best fields within each clan's allotment and, in consequence, had a more dependable food supply. Additional evidence for this explanation is provided by a comparison of ages among groups when the lineage of the spouse is taken into consideration. A person from a marginal lineage could improve his or her economic position significantly by marrying someone of a prime or alternate lineage regardless of rank. Only members of marginal lineages who married members of marginal lineages were significantly younger than all other combinations.

These findings draw our attention first to the economic importance of the lineage. Although the household was the primary productive unit, the fact that men of prime lineages often retained use rights to some of their sisters' fields further illustrates the lineage's corporate nature. The second point of interest is that the integrative function of the several rules of exogamy extends to the economic sphere as well as to the realm of social and ceremonial status.

Other signs of economic benefit deserve comment, although there are too few data available to warrant drawing conclusions. Eggan (personal communication, 1989) is of the opinion that high-status families were the first to get wagons and to earn cash by transporting goods from Winslow for the school and trader. There is also the possibility that rank had something to do with who herded livestock. Titiev's census listed 118 men who owned sheep and 15 who owned cattle. There was no relationship between livestock activities and either rank of clan or lineage position. Generally, the pavansinom were not visibly more wealthy. Neither their homes nor their personal belongings were obviously more opulent. What benefits accrued to them derived from their more secure position vis à vis their control of the best fields in a marginal environment and, of course, from their central positions in the political-religious structure.

Although cotton no longer played as significant a role in the Hopi economy during the latter half of the nineteenth century as it had in earlier times when the Hopis exported it to Zuni and the Rio Grande pueblos, it continued to be a trade item throughout the century (Hammond and Rey 1966:184–85; Kent 1983:13–14). Hopi cotton was grown as an annual and was adapted to the cool climate and short growing season of the area (Lewton 1913). The cotton plant requires a tremendous amount of water and did best in the floodplains and well-irrigated fields. In consequence, the clans controlling the best-quality fields were those best able to grow cotton as well as corn. During wet periods the competition between corn and cotton for the best-watered land was less intense than during periods of drought. Those clans with extensive fields on the floodplain of the Orayvi Wash were probably able to produce cotton except during the worst prolonged droughts. During the nineteenth century, cotton was traded to other pueblos and to Navajos, Apaches, and Havasupais for meat, hides, and luxury items such as turquoise and shell ornaments. It seems likely that the high-ranked clans benefited the most from this trade but that, by the time detailed ethnographic descriptions were made, cotton production was sufficiently curtailed that economic differences between high- and low-ranked clans were not observable.

Households, Lineages, Clans, and Phratries

The foregoing discussion leaves several questions unanswered: (1) Does the rank of a clan confer status on all its members equally, or is it only the prime and alternate lineages that embody the clan's "power" and position? (2) What is the relationship among the clans within a phratry, and to what extent can they share the position of the ranking clan by claiming its symbols? (3) What is the relationship among the households, the basic productive units, within a lineage or clan, and how "corporate" is the lineage? (4) To what degree is an individual's status determined by birth into a clan or lineage, and how much can an individual advance himself? These questions involve an understanding of Hopi kinship and social organization as well as social stratification.

The Hopi clan is a named consanguineal kin group composed of people united through the female line and thought to be descended from a common ancestor. Because of this, members of the same clan are considered to be genealogically related, although the actual links cannot be known. In Hopi theory clans and lineages are timeless, "stretching backward to the Emergence and continuing into the future. . . . While a Hopi distinguishes between 'own relatives' and 'clan relatives,' similar terms are extended to the latter, though on a somewhat simplified basis" (Eggan 1950:26–27). Most of the clans are represented on each mesa, if not in every village (see Eggan 1950:65–66), and, given the almost complete absence of intermesa marriage, it would be virtually impossible for clansmen from different mesas to be able to trace descent far enough into the past to discover actual genealogical relatedness.

Within a single village, however, the situation is somewhat different. In this instance a clan is composed of one or more matrilineages. Depending upon the size of the clan in that village, these lineages may or may not know how they are related to one another. To Eggan (1950:109), the lineage is of primary importance because it "contains the *mechanism* for transmitting rights, duties, land, houses, and ceremonial knowledge, and thus it is vital with respect to status."

Titiev introduced an element of confusion when he talked about a "household group" as a segment of a lineage. Lowie (1929:330) had defined a matrilineage as a group of matrilineally related kin descended from a common, known ancestress, and found between one and five distinct lineages in each named clan. Titiev recognized that there are lineages within a clan but believed that

> there is a smaller, distinct unit of consanguineous kin which functions actively, among other things, in the control and hereditary transmission of ceremonial offices and paraphernalia. . . . This unit is . . . none other than that segment of a matrilineal lineage which I have termed a household. . . . The basic feature of this grouping is the fact that a mature woman, her daughters, and occasionally, her granddaughters occupy a common residence through life and bring up their children under the same roof. (Titiev 1944:46)

Calling these lineage segments "households," or "household groups," creates confusion because a descent group is conflated with a residential group. Whiteley, for example, has trouble seeing how these "lineage segments" operate:

> Emphasis upon the lineage as basic is best regarded as an anthropological model rather than a full reflection of the empirical situation. . . . Which is the primary unit—lineage or clan? What if the two are empirically identical and occupy a single household? (Whiteley 1988:48–51)

Though a small clan may consist of a single household, this is true in only a few instances. Many clans comprised a single lineage as it has been defined by Lowie, and the larger clans comprised several lineages. The concept of descent from a known ancestor operates across generations, while the actual function of the lineages—as prime, alternate, or marginal—works to rearrange the status of the lineages and lineage segments within a single generation. In effect, lineage composition is almost constantly in a state of flux. Figure 4 shows how lineage position changes over the generations. For analytical purposes, what Titiev has called the lineage segment, or household group, is referred to here as the lineage, while the larger lineage may be thought of as a maxilineage.

In a single generation, the clan mother is the head of the prime lineage. Her sisters head alternate lineages, and her brothers are in the prime lineage because they are all able to take on the priestly offices of

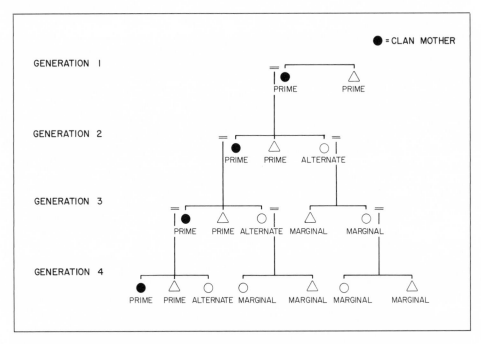

Figure 4. Prime, alternate, and marginal lineages.

the clan. As long as the clan mother lives, all her children are in the prime lineage. After one of her daughters succeeds to her position, however, the other daughters become heads of alternate lineages. Their cousins, the daughters of the alternate lineage heads of the previous generation, become members of a marginal lineage. Should none of the daughters of a clan mother survive to take over the position, a woman of an alternate lineage would do so. Because the lineage segments differ in their relationships to the clan mother they must be viewed as the functioning units.

The fact that the households of a lineage were often found scattered about the village rather than in close physical proximity may also obscure the functioning of lineages. Two factors work against the co-residence of the households in a lineage. The first is the simple fact that masonry architecture is not very flexible, so that as the extended family grows it must find living space elsewhere in the village. This contrasts with the Navajo pattern, for example, where another dwelling can always be built in close proximity to the several already in existence and where extended families are residence units. Among the Hopi, however, traditional architecture imposes constraints over time. In one generation, the households of two sisters may be next door to each other, each containing a married daughter and her family. In the next generation, the second and third married daughters of the sisters are forced to find living space elsewhere.

The second factor is that of *nawipti*, the ideal held by Hopis of establishing an independent household. Residence after marriage is, of course, matrilocal, keeping married daughters and their families with their mothers. But each daughter wishes to establish her own household. When she does so, space is made available for younger sisters to bring their husbands into the natal household. The couple lives matrilocally only long enough to "bond" the in-marrying male to his wife's family. This bonding is important because the relationships among the households of a lineage do not depend solely on coresidence. In the event that a clan mother dies after the daughter she has chosen to succeed her has already established a new household, that daughter will move back into her mother's house. The lineage responsibility overrides the place of residence, and any younger married daughters still in the clan house will have to leave.

In 1900, nuclear families comprised 54 percent of all households; matrifocal extended families 24 percent; couples without children 8 percent; and other combinations 13 percent. Female heads of nuclear family households were, on average, significantly younger (31.6 years) than those of extended families (42.3 years).[10] The seemingly high proportion of nuclear families is due primarily to the developmental cycle and is not much different from what has been found among the matrilineal Navajo at various times and in various parts of the reservation (table 3.5). Nor can one infer that matrilineal organization is weakened by the presence of neolocal nuclear households: In one pastoral area of the western Navajo reservation, for example, 40 percent of the residential units (camps) were neolocal despite the fact that less than 5 percent had established neolocal residence immediately after marriage (Levy, Henderson, and Andrews 1989).

Another aspect of the Hopi household that may cause confusion is the fact that it is not a residence and economic unit pure and simple. The men of the lineage, although they leave their natal household after

TABLE 3.5

HOPI HOUSEHOLD AND NAVAJO CAMP COMPOSITION (IN PERCENTAGES)

Community	Neolocal Nuclear	Extended	Other
Orayvi, 1900	54	24[a]	22
Navajo reservation, 1936–40[b]	53	47	—
Land Management District 17, 1936	55	—	—
Land Management District 2, 1936	49	—	—

[a] All of these are matrifocal extended families.
[b] Source for all Navajo entries is Henderson and Levy (1975:138). "Extended" includes all household forms; e.g., matrifocal, patrifocal, mixed, and other.

marriage, retain important functions within it at the same time as they assume new ones in their wives' households. A man must help discipline and educate his sisters' children, as well as perform a variety of ceremonial functions if his is a prime or alternate lineage. Even the economic lines may become blurred: a boy may be given some rights and duties with respect to land belonging to his natal household, "and he may continue to cultivate such a parcel after marriage" (Brandt 1954:19). If a male Soyal officer is assigned a plot of Bear clan land— although he may farm his wife's fields, the produce from which goes to her household—he will also farm his ceremonial plot, with some of its produce going to his sisters. In sum, the relationships among households are governed by what Eggan (1949) has called the lineage "principle," despite the fact that the lineage may be less important among the lower-ranked clans and marginal lineages in general.

Though data on field allocations are lacking, the significant differences among lineages in respect to age, fertility, and children's survival rates suggest that the lineage has some empirical substance, especially as lineages managed the non-partible clan property—the clan house, its ceremony and attendant offices, and its fields.[11]

We have seen that clan populations varied widely, some being as small as a single household and others comprising several lineages. In Orayvi there were nine maxilineages in six clans which had no known genealogical connection with the other lineages of the clan. Of 376

adults whose lineage position could be determined, 44 percent belonged to prime or alternate lineages. For clans with no clan lands and
no ceremonial position, lineage position meant little; all members were
of low status and, because there was neither land nor position to control, there was little to make genealogical distance from the clan mother
important. Among the smaller high-status clans, however, lineage position was important, although few of these clans' members were in
marginal lineages. Of the 12 adult members of Bear clan, for example,
only 3 belonged to marginal lineages; Spider clan, with 10 adults, had
only prime and alternate lineages; and Kyel (Hawk), with 6 adults, was
also composed entirely of prime and alternate lineages. In these smaller
high-status clans an individual was considered to be of high rank because of the possibility that the prime lineage might die out and other
lineages would then take its place. The determination of the proper heir
in these clans was made among so few candidates that no lineage was
completely alienated.

Among the larger clans of high and middle rank, however, the
position of individuals and lineages was less assured. The more distant
from the prime lineage, the less chance an individual had of inheriting
a ceremonial position. How he or she was regarded in the village depended largely on individual behavior and general deportment. The
marginal lineages of these clans had little chance for their members to
take over the positions controlled by the prime lineage, and they may
also have been marginal in respect to land if, like Spider clan, the clan
did not have large holdings on the floodplain. It is possible that some
people were thought of as commoners regardless of the rank of their
clan, although several Hopis dispute this. In the case of the high-ranked
clans, however, the problem did not arise because the only large clan
was Patki, which had extensive landholdings on the floodplain. For
large middle-ranking clans like Greasewood, with a population of 73,
the marginal lineages, whether thought of as pavansinom or not, were
most probably land hungry.

The relationship of lineages to the clan lands is one that cannot be
settled definitely at this late date. Whiteley contends that the "supposed" clan lands were very small in relation to Orayvi's population and
that in most instances only the prime lineage farmed the clan lands.
"Other clan members simply farmed in a large 'free area' in the Oraibi

valley" (Whiteley 1988:56). Yet, as we have seen, the clans with allotted lands on the floodplain had more than twice the acreage necessary for subsistence, and the remaining acreage on tributary fans and side valley slopes was large enough to provide a minimum acreage for the rest of the population. Surely, those clans with plenty of land would not demand that their marginal lineages farm in the free area. If that were so, there would have been a severe land shortage at Orayvi even during good times: The "large free area" comprised approximately 135 acres, only enough to provide for about 65 people.[12] Most of these fields were dependent on direct precipitation and were thus of poor quality and in need of lying fallow every few years.

The importance of the lineage, it seems to me, was in defining the order of succession to the control of clan property; the genealogical relationships becoming less important as the clan was less important or as the size of the clan increased. Without such ordering, conflicts among close relatives would arise too easily for the maintenance of social harmony.

Let us turn now to the relationships among clans of the same phratry, for here too I think we find a similar principle of succession at work. The phratry is a group of "linked" or associated clans:

> The phratry has no separate name, but it is nevertheless an important institution in Hopi life. The constituent clans are normally not considered to be descendents from a common ancestor but to have become "partners" as the result of common experiences during the mythical wanderings following the emergence. Kinship is extended to all the clans comprising the phratry—it is thus the largest unit in kinship extension. The phratry is also the largest exogamic unit, marriage being forbidden with all clans in the phratry group. The phratry, on the other hand, has no economic functions and does not act as a ritual unit, nor does it have any political duties. It does serve to tie clan units together into larger structures and furnishes a mechanism for dealing with clan extinction, since "partner" clans normally take over the ceremonial obligations. There also develop rivalries between clans within the phratry which may cause serious trouble and even disorganization. (Eggan 1950:62–63)

Of the nine phratries at Orayvi, five comprised three clans, two comprised only two clans, and the remaining two comprised four and five clans. Generally, one clan in each phratry was preeminent. In several, however, the clans were of equal rank. Several clans in Orayvi were on the verge of extinction. One, the Snake clan, had only six members, and its functions were being assumed by its phratry mate, the Lizard clan. By 1932, Kennard (n.d.) listed only Lizard clansmen, and even those individuals who had been members of Snake clan were remembered as Lizards. In this instance, the replacing clan did not assume the name of the clan that owned the key ceremony.

Although Parrot clan was not in immediate danger of dying out, a number of Crow clansmen were claiming to be Parrots at the turn of the century. Parrot, of course, was a high-ranking clan with a plot of Bear clan land in addition to its own allotment. Crow clan, on the other hand, was landless and had no ceremonial functions. Eggan lists Crow clan as "recently extinct" on all the mesas (Eggan 1950). At Orayvi, there were 31 Crow/Parrots of all ages in 1900. Of the 13 adult Crow/Parrot women at Orayvi, as many as 8 were Crows. Of the 10 men, perhaps 5 were Crows. All the Crows were hostile during the split and left Orayvi, which suggests that they had not been fully accepted and had certainly not replaced the Parrots. The crow is a despised animal among the Hopi because it ravages the corn crop, so perhaps in claiming to be Parrots the Crows were trying to avoid negative labeling. It is equally likely, however, that they were making an attempt to gain access to better land.

The conflict between the Patki and Piikyas clans described by Titiev (1944:201–2) was clearly over land. Patki, we recall, had extensive landholdings on the floodplain of the main wash, as well as two plots of Bear clan land in return for its service as Patki chief and Ahöla impersonator in the Soyal ceremony. With a population of 36 it was one of the larger clans, but it had no shortage of land. Its partner clan, Piikyas, on the other hand, was an even larger clan with 45 people and only very poor-quality fields. Piikyas claimed that Patki had come into possession of the Bear clan plot of land when Patki clan had taken over the Soyal function *from* Piikyas at a time when that clan had no adult heir able to assume the position. When the heirs reached maturity, Patki clan refused to give up its position and its claim to the plot of land. Because, however, the Patki clan fields on the wash were not in dispute, it is likely that Patki was always the preeminent clan of the phratry and Piikyas staked its claim on the fact that its *wu'ya* (clan symbol), corn, was as important as that of Patki, which was water. If Piikyas had once held the Soyal office, they more likely would have had the father of the minor heirs assume the position as regent rather than allowing another clan to take over from them.

In any event, Loololma, who was kikmongwi at the time, was irritated with the whole matter because, as he said, Patki held even more land than he did. He then decided to appoint the Piikyas clan to be his real helpers in the Soyal, a decision that gave Piikyas access to good land but did not deprive Patki of its own clan holdings. Information on the role of each clan in the Soyal is contradictory, however. Patki is said to have performed the Soyal function of impersonating the Ahöla katsina and participating in the chiefs' talk (Titiev 1944:62–63; Voth 1901:110–15). Titiev (1944:142) also assigned the function to Piikyas, and Voth (Dorsey and Voth 1901:12–13) lists Piikyas men as "chief assistants" in 1893 and 1899.

During the years preceding and following the Orayvi split, Kookop clan claimed Maasaw, the wu'ya of its phratry mate, Maasaw clan, and on this basis claimed to have come out of the *sipaapuni* (place of emergence) first and to be the rightful owner of all Orayvi lands (Yava 1978:52–53).

In the realm of principle, both lineages and phratry mates take over responsibilities as other clans or prime lineages die out. In Hopi thought, the clan is eternal, yet we have seen that clans do become extinct and that the succession is often attended by conflict.[13]

The tendency for competition to exist among clans may even be seen at the level of the individual in his efforts to attain respect and status. Although born into a clan and a lineage that place constraints upon the status that may be attained by individuals, both men and women could strive to improve their social position. A woman, tied to fields which might be of the poorest quality, could gain respect in the ceremonial sphere by being active in one of the women's societies. Economic position could be enhanced somewhat, although not radically changed, by her or her son's marriage to a spouse of high status. Her sisters-in-law would gift and feast her household in their role of father's sisters, and she would gift and feast her son's children. These relationships brought the lower-status woman into closer contact with better-placed families, and some economic benefit may be inferred from the age differences among women of different ranks and lineages.

Men strove to be industrious in order to attract women of higher rank as mates; as husbands, they shared in the economic benefits derived from farming better fields. Men, however, also directed their attention to the ceremonial sphere. A boy's chances for a better ceremonial position were enhanced by choosing a well-placed ceremonial father who would have him initiated into prestigious ceremonial societies, and marriage into a ceremonially important family increased his access to the society controlled by his wife's clan. Industriousness and religious participation, though they enhanced a man's individual status in the village, did not, however, raise him into the pavansinom.

With the decline of agriculture and the control of this resource by clans, the aspirations of individuals were less constrained by birth, and status came to be seen as directly related to material well-being. Speaking of the contemporary situation, in which wage work is the major source of income, Brandt (1954:27–28) says

> The Hopi definitely look up to a materially prosperous person. They are aware of the desirability of improving one's economic position. Many Hopi are quite energetic in improving their situation, for instance, by building more modern homes. And many Hopi are proud of the progress they have made since they were children. . . . The informant was asked, "Who are the high class Hopi?" F answered: "The people who have more things."

In sum, the Hopi system of stratification, although based on an inequitable distribution of the primary resource, functioned to manage scarcity rather than economic surplus. To do this, an ideology that gave sacred sanction to the status quo and emphasized the importance of every individual, clan, and ceremony was maintained; at the same time, a hierarchy of ceremonial status was recognized and accepted. The benefits accruing to persons of high status were security during times of drought—they were not the ones forced to migrate—and, possibly, better living conditions for those who survived childhood. There were, of course, the less tangible rewards of ceremonial preeminence. The means for preserving the resource and the descent group involved the support of preeminent clans by phratry mates, and support of the prime lineage that controlled the clan's resources and position by alternate and even more marginal lineages. Thus, despite competition and conflict, the central core of the clan and its resources was supported by ever-widening circles of related but essentially marginal clans and constituent lineages. Just how these marginal groups were tied to the center involved not only a conviction that the very survival of the society depended on it, but also some structurally integrative institutions that gave marginal individuals some access to the center. It is to a consideration of these mechanisms that we shall turn our attention in the next chapter.

CHAPTER 4

Social Integration

Hopi society, according to eggan (1950:116), "has been held together by kinship ties, marriage bonds, and associational structures which cut across clan lines." If the bonds of clan and lineage tend to be exclusive and often to work at cross-purposes to village integration, the counterforce must be sought in those institutions that cut across these lines. Among the Hopi, the choice of a marriage partner is, in theory, left to chance; this and the various rules of exogamy decrease the opportunities for clans or lineages to make alliances over time and thus promote the integration of the village. Similarly, the ceremonial societies which draw their membership from among all the clans provide men the opportunity to make alliances beyond those of clan and lineage. In this chapter, we consider the extent to which these institutions actually performed this integrative function.

Marriage

Descriptions of Hopi marriage practices are conflicting. According to Eggan (1975), alliance through preferential marriage and exchange was not used to perpetuate the status hierarchy, and marriage was often used to enhance the status of a household or of an individual; that is, as a means of upward mobility rather than as a way to preserve the position of specific clans or lineages. Brandt (1954:25), on the other hand, reports that the chiefs' families preferred to intermarry and that "it was seldom that a commoner married into the 'blue-blood' families." Furthermore, Eggan (1950:113) notes that marital ties were weak, because "where primary loyalties have developed to lineage and household it is difficult to develop strong ties between spouses, particularly with matrilocal residence and female ownership of house and land."

Aberle (1980) has described the contradictory forces at work in societies with unilineal descent as the relationships that pertain among kinsmen as opposed to those created by alliance through marriage. Affinal relationships are often difficult because one's in-laws, although not kinsmen and thus in some sense "outsiders," are at the same time close relatives of one's children, providing them with stable and enduring aid and support. "Marriage to kinsfolk outside one's unilineal unit who are as closely related as possible reduces the tensions of affinity, because marriage occurs between persons already connected. For that reason, people value marriage to relatives just beyond the border established by the exogamic rule" (Aberle 1980:134).

Such marriages were preferred among societies with unilineal descent whose communities were small. We have had occasion to remark that marriages into father's clan or phratry, and marriages between those whose fathers are of the same clan or phratry, were preferred by the Western Apaches and that, in all likelihood, Hopi society was similarly organized prior to A.D. 1300. But if settlements grow, as did the Hopi villages when they relocated to the southern edge of Black Mesa, so do the number of exogamous clans and phratries. Gough has suggested that "the larger the number of descent groups, the more rigorous in character and the more comprehensive in range will be the patrilateral marriage prohibitions" in societies with matrilineal descent (Gough 1961:619). It becomes necessary

> in territorial political units structured predominantly or entirely through kinship, for a large proportion of the unit's population to be linked by kinship ties for which customary rights and obligations are prescribed. . . . If there is a large number of descent groups in the relevant territorial unit, permission to marry back

into the father's group would mean permission to form small knots of closely in-marrying groups within the larger political unit, thus leaving the larger unit without a firm basis for structuring its relations as a whole. (Gough 1961:615)

The Hopis restricted marriage into (1) one's own clan and phratry, (2) father's clan and phratry, (3) shared father's clan and phratry, (4) mother's father's clan and phratry. Given the nine exogamous phratries at Orayvi, these prohibitions would allow marriage into less than half of the types of mates present in the village (Aberle 1980:131). In sum, the rules of exogamy served to promote village integration, forcing clans and lineages to make marriage alliances with groups not already allied in the prior generation. The extent to which marriage practices were successful in curbing any tendency for high status lineages to prefer making alliances with lineages of similar rank will be assessed by examining village endogamy, divorce, marriage within and across social strata, and rules of exogamy.

Village Endogamy

The man who married and went to live with a woman from another mesa could not fulfill his ceremonial obligations to his matrilineage, nor did he have kinship or ceremonial affiliations in his wife's village. The woman who went to live in her husband's village forfeited her interest in farmlands controlled by her matrilineage in order to live with a man who could not inherit productive land in his own village. In the endogamous marriage, though, both sets of relatives had some interest in helping the young couple adjust to married life. By contrast, the family of the man who had made an intermesa marriage might even want him to return home, while that of the bride could blame the son-in-law for any marital disagreements and might even create a climate conducive to marital discord. The children of such marriages would, in consequence, be reared in a stressful atmosphere and would be in a socially anomalous position due to the fact that the family of one of the parents would be unable to fulfill its many obligations to the children.

Insofar as possible, for the present study only marriages contracted prior to the Orayvi split were counted. Analyses of first marriages are presented because the patterns of subsequent marriages do not differ appreciably. Titiev examined all marriages listed in his household census regardless of when they took place. In consequence, the numbers of individuals and marriages he analyzed are always greater than those presented here.

Orayvi in 1900 was almost entirely endogamous. Of the 284 adult women listed in Titiev's household census, only four had not been born in Orayvi. Two of these in-marrying women came from other mesas; two were Navajo. Of the Orayvi women, only five married outsiders. Of 282 adult men, five were from outside, three from Second Mesa, one from Haano, and one was Navajo. Five Orayvi men had married outsiders. There were, then, only 10 Orayvi men and women who had entered into what must have been considered undesirable unions, and it is of some interest to speculate on what sort of people they were.

None of the out-marrying men and only one of the women came from a high-ranking clan. With the exception of the Bow clan woman, who belonged to a prime lineage, and a Gray Badger man, all were from marginal lineages. After Humihongqa's (Bow clan woman) first Navajo husband died, she married another Navajo. There is no comment on this in Titiev's census, but the lineage is an interesting one. Her two brothers, both of whom became Al society chiefs, were insane. The older generation had been in the Hostile faction prior to the split, and the village chief's reaction to this is reflected in the version of the creation myth he related to Voth, which will be discussed in the final chapter. Thus, the general pattern is that commoners occasionally married outsiders, but in the single instance of a member of a prime lineage from a high-ranking clan doing so, some form of deviance was present in the family.

The position of an individual marrying into the village was difficult. None of the in-marrying men ever joined a ceremonial society, despite the fact that four were from other Hopi mesas and had been initiated. The situation may have been different for the women, perhaps because of the importance of women in determining descent. Tuvenömqa, a Navajo woman, became the "mother" of a new clan (Navajo Badger), and although she never joined a society, her daughters did.

The woman from Haano joined no societies and returned to Haano with her son after the death of her husband. A Second Mesa woman, who died some time before the split, joined Powamuy, but there is no information about any children. No information is given on the other in-marrying woman.

Divorce

Divorce is said to have been frequent: "marriages . . . are essentially unstable, and . . . Hopi monogamy is of a very brittle order indeed" (Titiev 1944:40). As we have seen, Eggan attributes this to the conflict between loyalty to the natal household and loyalty to the spouse. But Eggan appears to be referring to the effects factional divisions have on marriage:

> Alliances between clans are continually developing out of common ceremonial activities or in terms of control of kiva groups. Where there is a persuasive leader such alliances may form the basis for factions, and if continued over a long enough period are frequently strengthened by intermarriage. Conversely, spouses in different factions may be encouraged to separate. This is possibly the reason for the very high divorce rate Titiev found for Old Oraibi and the fact that when the split came households went or remained as units. (Eggan 1975:283)

The questions posed by these characterizations are, first, What is a high divorce rate and, second, What was the divorce rate in Hopi society undisturbed by the factioning that culminated in the split of 1906? In regard to the first, separation and divorce are remarkably culture specific, which makes comparative studies virtually impossible. In some societies legal obstacles to obtaining a divorce can be very great, in others virtually nonexistent. After some of the restrictions on divorce were relaxed in England in 1970, the divorce rates rose precipitously. In many countries divorce is inhibited by the economic dependence of women on their husbands and the divorce rates may rise as the economic position of women improves. In Hopi society women were secure in their ownership of house and land and in the custody of their children. In addition, there were no formal barriers to divorce. What then would a high divorce rate be? As to the second question, it is impossible to reconstruct divorce rates prior to the development of factions during the late nineteenth century, so one can only speculate on the effects of factional loyalties.

Keeping these caveats in mind, we may look at the proportion of divorced women in Orayvi.[1] Titiev based his calculations on the marital histories of 423 women. These included marriages made by women already deceased by 1900 as well as by women who reached adulthood and made their marriages after the 1906 split. He found 35 percent to have been divorced at least once. I excluded virtually all of the marriages made after 1906 and also excluded women who separated and remarried after 1906, as well as those whose marital histories appeared to be incomplete and those who were deceased by 1900. This did not yield a different divorce rate: 31 percent of 147 adult women alive in 1900 had been divorced and remarried at least once.[2] This rate appears high in comparison with comparable rates from present-day United States. In 1960, only 4 percent of all women ever married in the U.S. were divorced. By 1980, this figure had risen to 10.7 percent. Estimates of future trends suggest that of marriages made in 1952, 32.1 percent are likely to end in divorce; for marriages made in 1962, 40 percent, and for those made in 1972, 49.2 percent (Hacker 1983:110–12). Clearly, it depends on one's point of reference whether the Hopi divorce rate is thought to be high or about average.

The question remains, however, whether or not divorce was promoted by conflicts of loyalties between lineages and affines. Titiev's field notes contain accounts of marriages that were dissolved because of different factional allegiances. Yet of the 45 divorced women only three had divorced men belonging to the opposing faction. If these cases are disregarded, the divorce rate would still be 28.6 percent. I am inclined to agree with Titiev's judgment that the rates were high and that the causes of divorce were more in the realm of personal choice than in specific structural pressures. Considering the secure position of Hopi women, however, I am also of the opinion that marriage was not more fragile among the Hopi than it is in other societies that place few constraints or penalties and allowed individuals more opportunity to follow their personal desires.

Marriage Within and Across Social Strata

We turn now to the question of whether the pavansinom preferred to marry within their own class. Several things worked to prevent this from happening, in addition to the rules of exogamy already mentioned. The first is that marriage of a previously married person to one not yet married—a practice known as "basket-carrier" marriage—was frowned upon and, after death, the offender (the person who had been married before) was forced to carry a heavily loaded basket on his or her back from the grave to the land of the dead (Titiev 1944:36). This tended to restrict first marriages to those within one age cohort, say between 18 and 24 years of age. If the prime lineages of high-ranking clans preferred to make alliances within this small group, the number of available mates would be small indeed, especially when the rules of exogamy are applied. The second is the differing needs of men and women when considering the choice of a mate.

Women in a matrifocal household need husbands to farm their lands and thus look favorably on industrious young men regardless of their status. Women also gain sisters-in-law and become sisters-in-law to their brothers' wives' households. The affinally related households engage in a considerable amount of reciprocal exchange of food and clothing and assist one another on all the occasions when cornmeal is to be ground or *piiki* (a paper-thin cornmeal bread) made (Eggan 1975: 280). Thus, a high-ranking women looks for an industrious, lower-ranked husband whose sisters gain relationships with high-ranking sisters-in-law, and the interests of both high- and low-ranking households coincide. The major interest of high-ranking Hopi men, however, is in the ceremonial system, and marriage into key households and induction into the proper kiva ceremonial groups offer the major means of achieving higher ceremonial position. In effect, lower-status men and women desire to marry into higher-ranking households, and in this their desires coincide with the desire for high-status households to attract good workers. In consequence, the high-status males compete with lower-status males for the same mates.

Women, in fact tend to marry down, although the pattern just misses statistical significance (table 4.1). There was even less association between marriage and rank for men.

TABLE 4.1

| Woman's Rank | Husband's Rank | | | | | | Totals |
| | High | | Middle | | Low | | |
	Obs[a]	(Exp)[b]	Obs	(Exp)	Obs	(Exp)	
High	3	(9.89)	29	(25.46)	18	(14.65)	50
Middle	34	(26.31)	63	(67.72)	36	(38.97)	133
Low	17	(17.8)	47	(45.82)	26	(26.37)	90
Totals	54		139		80		273

Note: Chi-square = 8.934; df = 4; p = .063 (not significant).
[a]Obs = Observed.
[b](Exp) = Expected.

Rules of Exogamy

Titiev recorded 16 men who had married into their father's clan and 27 who had married into their father's phratry. Fewer women made such marriages: 2 into father's clan and 17 into father's phratry. Although he did not calculate rates for these prohibited marriages, Titiev concluded that "insofar as recent times are concerned, matings with members of the father's clan and phratry are readily condoned" (Titiev 1944:36). We recall, first, that marriage into father's clan and phratry is a means by which alliances may be made among a small group of intermarrying clans, and second, that Titiev was including marriages that were contracted after the split, when the population of each faction was only half of that of the village prior to the split—a circumstance that may have so restricted the choice of mates that the traditional prohibitions could no longer be observed.

By restricting our analysis to first marriages contracted before 1906, we may get a better idea about the frequency of prohibited unions. One woman had married into her own phratry, and one man had married a woman of his own clan. This single case of clan incest involved members of the Sun clan; the woman had been married previously and the man was much younger than she was, making it a doubly disapproved union. The couple left the reservation subsequently. There was also one shared father's clan marriage noted in Titiev's census; a rare enough occasion for the village chief to comment on it and note that it never happened in "the old days."

Two women had married into father's clan, and 5 into father's phratry. Among men, there were 7 father's clan and 12 father's phratry marriages. Whether these marriages were readily condoned, as Titiev believed, cannot be determined. When compared with similar marriages made among Navajo women of the Kaibito Plateau between 1880 and 1914, however, the rates do not seem excessive (table 4.2). About 4.3 percent of Hopi women's and 12.5 percent of Hopi men's marriages were to spouses of father's clan or phratry, as compared to 14.5 percent of the Navajo women's marriages (Levy, Henderson, and Andrews 1989).

A disproportionate number of these marriages were to men and women in the Maasaw phratry, especially to Kookop clan. Of the 7 women, 6 married into Maasaw phratry, and 4 of these were to Kookop men. Of the 19 men, 8 married into Maasaw phratry, and 2 of these were to Kookop women. Although Titiev did not report on the patterning of this type of marriage, he was impressed with the fact that 6 of the 12 women who had made "basket-carrier" marriages were members of Maasaw phratry (Titiev 1944:37).

TABLE 4.2

MARRIAGES OF HOPIS AND NAVAJOS BY TYPE (IN PERCENTAGES)

Type	Navajo Women		Hopi Women		Hopi Men	
	%	N	%	N	%	N
Clan						
Own	0.0	236	0.0	273	0.4	264
Father's	5.3	206	1.2	163	4.6	151
Phratry						
Own	0.0	236	0.4	273	0.0	264
Father's	9.2	206	3.1	163	7.9	151

Source: Levy, Henderson, and Andrews 1989.
N = Number of marriages in each category with sufficient information for analysis.

Titiev believed that marriage into father's clan or phratry was a survival from an earlier time when this form of marriage was preferred, and earlier still when cross-cousin marriage was practiced (Titiev 1938). But, as we have seen, these forms of marriage were preferred prior to A.D. 1300, making it difficult to believe that the same reasons for contracting them had persisted into the nineteenth century. Among the Kaibito Plateau Navajos, over 50 percent of father's clan and phratry marriages were made by only 6 percent of the lineages in the area, and these lineages made such marriages over several generations. These were families with medium-size sheep holdings who needed to protect their claims to limited resources in open range by repeatedly marrying close neighbors. In effect, their situations were similar to those of the Western Apaches who preferred to make such marriages rather than let outsiders gain access to their limited farmlands. The point is simply that breaches of marriage restrictions occur for a reason and are not some sort of reflex imprinted in the distant past.

In the Hopi case the tendency for father's clan and phratry marriages to involve clans of the Maasaw phratry implicates the factional split as a reason for making prohibited alliances. Because Kookop was the leading clan of the Hostile faction, the political allegiance of its phratry mates became a matter of concern. Maasaw was a high-ranking clan which, should it have gone over to the Hostiles, would have weakened the village chief's faction considerably. Many Coyote clansmen were undecided about their allegiance until almost the last minute. Marriages into Maasaw, Coyote, and Water Coyote clans were made most often by members of the chief's party. I believe these were political alliances and not efforts to make persisting alliances for reasons of status and economic benefit.

In balance, marriage alliances tended to integrate the body politic by uniting households of different rank. Rules of exogamy prohibited the creation of cliques. This is not to say that the chiefs' families would not have preferred to do so if it had been possible and if the need for farm labor had not made it desirable to marry down. Hopi statements quoted by Brandt (1954:25) seem to represent the desired rather than the actual state of affairs. Among contemporary Hopis the children of "deviant" marriages are those most at risk to become alcoholics or commit suicide.[3] These include children not only from the intermesa and

First Mesa marriages between Hopis and Hopi-Tewas but also those between the highest- and lowest-ranked clans (Levy and Kunitz 1987; Levy, Kunitz, and Henderson 1987). In my opinion, this suggests that, although almost 20 percent of all marriages were between high- and low-status individuals and these did not end in divorce more frequently than other marriages, they were often more stressful.

CEREMONIAL ALLIANCES

Ceremonies and kivas are controlled by clans, and the priestly offices of the societies are filled whenever possible by members of the controlling clan. Because membership in the society responsible for performing the ceremony, and hence in the kiva housing it, is open to individuals regardless of clan, the ceremonial societies have been considered as a major integrating mechanism. According to Eggan, the membership actually cuts across the clan-phratry system:

> Since the "ceremonial father" is selected from an unrelated clan and since he initiates his "ceremonial son" into all the societies to which he belongs, the initiation procedure automatically brings about such a distribution of membership. . . . Curing and trespass are alternative paths to membership, and any adult may request a member to initiate him if he so desires. (Eggan 1950:91)

As Eggan reiterates, "the major horizontal strands holding Hopi society together are made up of the ceremonial societies" (Eggan 1975:282).

The major interest of men is in the ceremonial system, and society membership, like marriage, offers the means of achieving a higher ceremonial position (Eggan 1975:281). Yet it is also possible that alliances made among clans in a ceremonial society may serve to strengthen factional divisions and so work against village integration (Eggan 1975:283).[4] The first question, then, is whether the societies draw their membership from a broad range of clans and phratries; the second is the degree to which rank and lineage position affect membership in societies.

The women's societies include members of all clans and phratries (table 4.3).[5] The women who have positions in the men's societies come

TABLE 4.3

WOMEN'S SOCIETY MEMBERSHIP BY CLAN

Clan	Soyal	Powa-muy	Taw	Al	Kwan	Blue Flute	Gray Flute	Snake	Ante-lope	Mom-tsit	Maraw	Lakon	Oaqöl	Total
Bear	3	1									5	4		13
Spider	1					4					3			8
Katsin		2										1		3
Parrot	1	3									3	6	7	20
Rabbit		1									7	8	12	28
Snake								1			1			2
Lizard											11	3	8	22
Sand											6	8	18	32
Reed											16	1	8	25
Greasewood	1										4	6	5	16
Bow											7		1	8
Maasaw											7	7	10	24
Kookop											1			1
Coyote											12	8	7	27
Water Coyote											8	9	8	25
Millet													1	1

Clan	Soyal	Powa-muy	Taw	Al	Kwan	Blue Flute	Gray Flute	Snake	Ante-lope	Mom-tsit	Maraw	Lakon	Oaqöl	Total
Badger		6									7	7	10	30
Gray Badger		2									2	1	1	5
Navajo Badger											1			1
Butterfly														
Patki							3				2	2	5	12
Piikyas									1		12	1	16	30
Rabbitbrush														
Squash							1			1	1	1		4
Hawk							1				2	1	6	10
Crane												1	1	2
Sun											6	4	5	15
Eagle											2		2	4
Totals	6	15	0	0	0	4	5	1	1	1	126	78	131	368

Note: Clans grouped by phratry.

TABLE 4.4

MEN'S SOCIETY MEMBERSHIP BY CLAN

Clan	Soyal	Powa-muy	Taw	Al	Kwan	Blue Flute	Gray Flute	Snake	Ante-lope	Mom-tsit	Maraw	Lakon	Oaqöl	Total
Bear	5				1	2	1	1	1	1	1			10
Spider			1	1		6	1	1	3	7				18
Katsin		4	2	1	1		1							9
Parrot	1	8	3	2	1	1				1			1	18
Rabbit	3	2	1	3	1		2	3		1				16
Snake		1	1		1			4		1	1			8
Lizard				3	3		2	7		5	3			20
Sand		2	2	5	3	1	1		1	5				20
Reed		1		1	2	3	1	2		5	1			16
Greasewood	4		2	2	1	2	2	1		2				14
Bow	1	1		2		2	1							7
Maasaw	3			2	4		1	1		2				12
Kookop			2	3		2	1		2	7				17
Coyote	2	1	1	1	1		4			7				17
Water Coyote		1	2	1	1		1	4	1	3				13
Millet		1								1				1

Clan	Soyal	Powa-muy	Taw	Al	Kwan	Blue Flute	Gray Flute	Snake	Ante-lope	Mom-tsit	Maraw	Lakon	Oaqöl	Total
Badger	1	15	2	6	2		2	3	1	2				34
Gray Badger		15	4	3	4	2				1				29
Navajo Badger		4		1			1					1		7
Butterfly		1					1			1				3
Patki	1		2	2	1	4	8	2	3	2				25
Piikyas	3		1	4			1	1	1	1				11
Rabbitbrush				2			2							4
Squash							1							1
Hawk							1	1		1				3
Crane					1		2							3
Sun	1	1	1	2			1	1		1				8
Eagle		3	3	1			1	1						6
Totals	25	57	28	45	28	23	36	31	13	58	4	2	0	350

Note: Clans grouped by phratry.

mostly from the clans and phratries of the clans controlling those societies, and the same is true for the men who hold positions in the women's societies. In those cases where a woman holding office in a men's society (or a man in a women's) is not a member of the controlling clan or phratry, she or he is always the spouse of a member of the controlling clan or phratry. There are more men's societies and, in consequence, the membership in each is considerably smaller than in the women's societies (table 4.4). Nevertheless the membership is drawn from most, if not all, of the phratries. The Momtsit (War), Snake, and Gray Flute societies included members from all phratries in the village. There is, then, no tendency for a limited group of allied clans to predominate in any one society.

Powamuy, controlled by Badger and Katsin clans, drew 86 percent of its members from the clans of their respective phratries, while Momtsit, controlled by Spider and Kookop clans, drew half of its membership from the phratries of the controlling clans. More than two-thirds of the members of the majority of societies belonged to phratries that were not related to the controlling clans. To the extent that a man wished to enhance his status, he was given ample opportunity in the ceremonial sphere, and the societies may be considered as successful an integrating mechanism as marriage.

Lineage position was associated with the number of societies a woman joined. Regardless of clan rank, women of prime and alternate lineages tended to join more societies, and fewer joined no society than would have been expected by chance (table 4.5). A similar pattern was found among the men.[6] Both clan rank and lineage were strongly associated with the number of societies joined by men, when clans of the Badger phratry were left out of the analysis. Badger was the medicine animal and, ideally, a Badger served as the dispenser of medicines in every men's society. Although Badger clansmen are found in 9 of the 10 men's societies, other clans of the phratry, especially Gray Badger, are also distributed widely among the societies. By excluding these clans from consideration, one can control for the influence of their particular ceremonial function unrelated to the control of a ceremony by a single clan—a greater demand for the low-ranking clans of this phratry (table 4.6).

The possibility for members of low-ranking clans, or from marginal

TABLE 4.5
NUMBER OF SOCIETIES JOINED BY LINEAGE

Lineage	Number of Societies 0 Obs	(Exp)	1 Obs	(Exp)	2+ Obs	(Exp)	Total
Women[a]							
Prime/Alternate	11	(17.9)	30	(14.0)	51	(41.1)	92
Marginal	33	(26.1)	51	(48.0)	50	(59.9)	134
Totals	44		81		101		226
Men[b]							
Prime	4	(10.31)	38	(32.13)	29	(28.56)	71
Marginal	22	(15.69)	43	(48.67)	43	(43.44)	108
Totals	26		81		72		179

[a]Chi-square = 8.96; df = 2; p = .01.
[b]Chi-square = 8.19; df = 2; p < .02.

TABLE 4.6
NUMBER OF SOCIETIES JOINED BY MEN, BY RANK AND LINEAGE
(CLANS OF BADGER PHRATRY OMITTED)

	0 Obs	(Exp)	1 Obs	(Exp)	2+ Obs	(Exp)	Total
Rank[a]							
High	4	(8.51)	18	(23.18)	25	(15.31)	47
Middle	22	(18.46)	50	(50.31)	30	(33.23)	102
Low	14	(13.03)	41	(35.51)	17	(23.45)	72
Totals	40		109		72		221
Lineage[b]							
Prime/Alternate	4	(10.67)	35	(30.38)	23	(20.94)	62
Marginal	22	(15.32)	39	(43.62)	28	(30.06)	89
Totals	26		74		51		152

[a]Chi-square = 13.37; df = 4; p <.01.
[b]Chi-square = 8.62; df = 2; p = .01.

lineages of the large middle-ranking clans, to enhance their status by attaining a ceremonial office appears to have been limited. Lineage membership was important for both men and women; women of marginal lineages held offices significantly less often than women of prime and alternate lineages (table 4.7). Only 3 of 93 women of low rank held a ceremonial office, and all were from prime lineages. Two held office because of their husbands' positions. A Piikyas woman married to a

TABLE 4.7

CEREMONIAL OFFICES HELD, BY LINEAGE AND RANK

| | Number of Offices | | | | |
| | 0 | | 1–2 | | |
	Obs	(Exp)	Obs	(Exp)	Total
Women by Lineage[a]					
Prime/Alternate	88	(93.79)	14	(8.21)	102
Marginal	129	(123.21)	5	(10.79)	134
Totals	217		19		236
Woman by Rank[b]					
High	39	(42.15)	7	(3.85)	46
Middle	118	(118.21)	11	(10.79)	129
Low	84	(80.64)	4	(7.36)	88
Totals	241		22		263
Men by Lineage[c]					
Prime	45	(54.4)	27	(17.6)	72
Marginal	91	(81.6)	17	(26.4)	108
Totals	136		44		180
Men by Rank[d]					
High	32	(36.93)	15	(10.07)	47
Middle	92	(96.64)	31	(26.36)	123
Low	85	(75.43)	11	(20.57)	96
Totals	209		57		266

[a]Chi-square corrected for continuity = 6.52; df = 1; p = .01.
[b]Chi-square = 4.5; df = 2; p = .11 (not significant).
[c]Chi-square = 11.07; df = 1; p <.001.
[d]Chi-square = 9.78; df = 2; p <.01.

Bear clansman was a Soyalmana because of her husband's position and because her clan held an important office in Soyal. The clan mother of Sun clan was an officer in Lakon society. She was married to a Spider man, who was also a chief in the Antelope society. One woman may, however, have attained status by her own actions; of Reed clan, she held a minor office in Maraw and was married to a Lizard who held no offices and whose lineage is not known.

Eleven men of low rank also held ceremonial office. Two Piikyas men held office in Soyal. The Village chief, it will be recalled, put Piikyas into the Soyal in Patki's stead. Two Sun clansmen held office in Soyal because they were married to Bear women. Two Gray Badger and one Navajo Badger held office as medicine dispensers, positions that would go to clans in Badger phratry if Badgers were not available. One Kookop man was an officer in Momtsit, which was controlled by Kookop. Another served as War chief in the Blue Flute society by virtue of Kookop's warrior role. Blue Flute was controlled by Spider clan, which shared control of Momtsit with Kookop and was allied with this clan in the factional dispute. A third Kookop man was a Crier chief—but "not a real Crier," according to Titiev, and so may be discounted as holding a real ceremonial position. Only one man may have achieved position on his own. A Piikyas clansman, he was a member of Taw society and a "chief" in Antelope. He was married to a Coyote woman from a marginal lineage who was also active in the ceremonial life and belonged to all the women's societies, although she held no office. We do not know this man's lineage or whether his political affiliation was a factor.

In sum, although both marriage and the ceremonial sodalities worked to integrate the society and prevent the formation of cliques of high-ranking clans, they were not entirely successful. Rank and lineage were important factors in men's selection of mates, despite the tendency for women to marry men of lesser rank. Clan rank and lineage position were also positively associated with the number of societies an individual joined. Moreover, the upward mobility of individuals measured by the number of ceremonial offices held was severely limited; only one man and one woman of low-ranked clans held ceremonial office for reasons other than belonging to a clan that controlled the society or being married to a spouse of importance in the society. The "inherited" medicine power of the Badger clan also appears to have benefited the low-ranked clans in the Badger phratry, as their members joined many societies and held office in some.

Although an ideology emphasizing the importance of all Hopis and all ceremonial activities was probably an essential counterbalance to the divisiveness of social stratification, it is important to recognize that the integrative structural mechanisms were also an important ingredient. Opportunity for participation in the ceremonial life was sufficient to prevent the alienation of the common people under the normal conditions of life. Whether unusual stresses destroyed this balance along lines of the social strata will be examined in the following chapters, which analyze the fissioning of Orayvi in 1906.

CHAPTER 5

The

Disintegration of Orayvi

I N 1906, A FACTIONAL DISPUTE that had been brewing in Orayvi for over a quarter of a century culminated in the disintegration of the village. Almost all observers, including Hopis, agreed that the casus belli was a dispute over the appropriate response to United States policies regarding the Hopi. In consequence, the factions were initially referred to as Friendlies and Hostiles and, later, as Progressives and Conservatives. There has been considerably less agreement concerning the underlying causes of the dissention. Parsons (1922:283) and, more recently, Clemmer (1978:58) believe acculturative stress to have been both a necessary and a sufficient cause. Titiev (1944:63n27, 69) believed that the underlying causes of the split were a dispute over land coupled with the lack of any centralized political authority that could override loyalty to the clan. Bradfield (1971:36–37, 45) has proposed that with the erosion of the main wash, the growing population of the village came to exceed the carrying capacity of the agricultural land. Most recently, Whiteley (1988:289) has rejected these explanations and has proposed instead that we accept a Hopi explanation to the effect that the split was conceived and carried out by the leaders of both factions in concert as a fulfillment of an ancient prophecy—overpopulation, water shortages, and depletion of farmland notwithstanding.

Although the study of factions has engaged the attention of anthropologists since the 1960s, to date no unitary explanation has been found that satisfactorily accounts for them. One theme, however, appears to run through many studies done by political anthropologists; namely, that factionalism is "an emergent phenomenon accompanying the marginalization of rural communities during certain phases of State capitalism and the global economy" (Vincent 1978:188). This finding is not surprising in light of the fact that virtually all detailed studies of factions have been carried out among colonized societies many years after first contact with the industrialized West.

In contrast to the studies of factionalism by political anthropologists stand many ethnographic accounts of small societies which contain descriptions of intravillage conflict and village fissioning. These accounts usually identify the precipitating events leading to the split itself, which is always preceded by intravillage conflict and quarrels. But whether the causes of the split have anything to do with the subject of the dispute is not clear. Carneiro (1987) has proposed that factional divisions in *autonomous* villages tend to result in the splitting of the village and that this is often the direct consequence of population growth. In this view, factions and village fissioning are characteristic of the prehistoric world and are not just a consequence of conquest and the changes attendant upon the process of modernization.

The vast majority of North American Indian societies lacked political institutions with the power to integrate more than one village or even to override the powers of kinship groups to manage their own affairs (Jorgensen 1987:175); thus, they may have been prone to factionalism regardless of the causes of dissent. It is, of course, also arguable that aboriginal factionalism, pervasive as it may have been, was less destructive of community life because the pressures that gave rise to it were neither as persistent nor as threatening to sovereignty and survival as those faced by Indian communities since contact. If internal divisions and dissention existed before the conquest, it would be unwise to assume that factions observed in postcontact American Indian communities are always caused by stresses consequent upon conquest and pressures to acculturate.

In this context, it is important to note that many who have commented on factionalism among the Pueblo societies of the Southwest have recognized that it is not a recent phenomenon. Simmons (1979: 218), without giving his reasons, "infers" that "divisive particularism . . . endemic among the Pueblos throughout Spanish colonial times, . . . was equally prevalent in the precontact period. . . . In some cases a controversial issue split villages apart so that one faction voluntarily withdrew to found a new Pueblo or received asylum in another community." And Parsons (1922:283), while attributing the fissioning of Orayvi to the stresses of contact, notes that archaeological evidence suggests the process of village fissioning has been characteristic of Pueblo life for centuries.

In the Pueblo Southwest temporary or permanent schisms have occurred at San Juan, San Ildefonso, Santa Clara, Isleta, Cochiti, Zia, San Felipe, Acoma, Laguna, and Zuni. In some instances, as at Laguna (Simmons 1979:218), Santa Clara (Arnon and Hill 1979:302), Taos (Fenton 1957), and possibly Isleta (French 1948; Ellis 1979:362–63), the divisions were clearly responses to acculturative stress. At San Ildefonso, however, high mortality rates and declining prosperity were blamed by some on the late nineteenth-century relocation of the village to a more northerly location, when, according to tradition, the village should always be located to the south. The disaffected villagers then built a new village on the old site, and each village became an autonomous ceremonial unit (Edelman 1979:309–12).

Carneiro (1987) has suggested that various types of social organization make a village more or less likely to fission as the population grows. A village with moieties, despite the fact that the population is divided into halves, is more strongly integrated and able to accommodate a larger population than one with unilineal descent groups alone. We recall that both Titiev and Eggan have characterized the Hopi clan system as lacking in centralized political institutions and prone to factioning due to the self-interests of the clans. Eggan (1966:124, 127–28) suggests that the pueblos to the east of Hopi were better able to withstand the stresses of contact with Spaniards and Anglo-Americans because they had stronger centralized political controls. On the other hand, Dozier believes that factionalism among the Rio Grande Pueblos was made more likely by strong centralized government:

It is opposition to the compulsory dictates of the Pueblo authorities which has brought about dissatisfaction and discord in the past as well as at present. Forced participation in all communal activities and the prohibition of all deviant behavior, though designed to discourage the rise of dissident groups, have often had the opposite effect and have resulted in frequent factional disputes. (Dozier 1966:176)

By reviewing Hopi history we can see that environmental conditions as well as problems with the Spanish occupation of New Mexico may have contributed to the development of dissention between and within villages. It is also possible to detect some continuities in the ways Hopis responded to Spanish demands that reappear during the period of Anglo-American occupation.

The Spanish Period

We have had occasion to note that at the time of the first contact with the Spaniards in 1540, the Hopi were living in seven villages near four mesas—Awat'ovi and Kawaika by Antelope Mesa, Walpi and Sikyatki by First Mesa, Songoopavi and Musangnuvi by Second Mesa, and Orayvi at Third Mesa. According to Spicer (1962),[1] the Spaniards were never able to muster sufficient strength to missionize and dominate the Hopis, who were determined to pick and choose from among Spanish ideas and technologies while keeping the Spaniards at a distance. Throughout the Spanish period, drought and famine alternated with times of relative plenty, and resistance to Spanish demands alternated with acceptance and cooperation. The extent to which economic conditions influenced Hopi responses to Spanish proselytizing or either of these factors fostered village factioning and intervillage conflict is difficult to determine. Both exerted their influence at different times, however, and it would be a mistake to interpret Hopi history entirely in terms of economic or acculturative determinants.

When, in 1540, a party from the Coronado expedition first visited Hopi, the Spaniards were received with hostility. The visit was terminated when the village of Kawaika was attacked and partially destroyed. The village was soon abandoned, partly as a result of the destruction but also, in all likelihood, because of the failing water supply, which had been making life difficult in the Jeddito valley for some years. Sikyatki, by First Mesa, was also apparently abandoned at about this time, as it was uninhabited when the Espejo expedition arrived in 1583. The down-cutting of the Jeddito Wash, which watered the fields of the Antelope Mesa villages, was already well advanced, and four villages had been abandoned prior to the arrival of the Spaniards (Brew 1979:514; Hack 1942:55).

Water tables had been dangerously low since 1300, but they began to rise slowly after 1500, and relations with the Spaniards were relatively peaceful. Espejo had been received hospitably in 1583, as was Oñate in 1598, at which time the Hopis gave formal submission to the King of Spain. In 1614, Captain Marquez reported that the Hopis were living in five villages (Awat'ovi, Walpi, Songoopavi, Musangnuvi, and Orayvi) with a population of around 3,000. The Hopis and Zunis were regarded as the frontiers of New Mexico; no efforts were made at conversion until 1628, and both tribes were exempted from paying tribute.

In 1629, three missionaries were assigned to Hopi. The Hopis were cooperative and, under Franciscan direction, built three churches, one each at Awat'ovi, Songoopavi, and Orayvi, with *visitas* (small church structures with no resident priest) at Walpi and Musangnuvi. Although there were troubles—one missionary was poisoned in 1633 and complaints were lodged against another in 1655—the mission program proceeded. The Hopis refused, when asked, to join with Taos Pueblo in a plan for revolt in 1650, and they seem not to have had their kivas raided by the missionaries in the 1670s. There was a serious drought in 1659, when crops failed and food was sent to the Hopis from Santa Fe. Yet the Hopis supported the Pueblo Revolt of 1680 and killed the missionaries living among them.

Following the revolt, the Hopis hosted Eastern Pueblo refugees who feared Spanish reprisals. Refugees founded the Tewa village of Haano on First Mesa and Payupki on Second Mesa. It was also at this time that the Hopis, apprehensive about possible Spanish retaliation, moved their villages from near the springs at the base of the mesas to the mesa tops—Walpi to First Mesa, and Songoopavi and Musangnuvi to Second Mesa. In addition, Songoopavi established the new village of Supawlavi at a very inaccessible spot on Second Mesa where ceremonial paraphernalia could be hidden from the Spaniards. In 1692, the Hopis swore allegiance to de Vargas on condition that the Spaniards would not attack. Then, after further Eastern Pueblo uprisings in 1692 and 1696, even more refugees came to Hopi country and were allowed to settle in the new villages.

Noting the success of the Spanish reconquest of New Mexico, the Hopis were anxious not to renew hostilities. Just how this was to be accomplished, however, was not clear. On the one hand, some Hopis from Awat'ovi offered to rebuild their mission in 1699, and the three missionaries sent to Awat'ovi recommended that a garrison be posted to Hopi country to protect the Christianized Indians. On the other hand, another group of Hopis went to Santa Fe in 1700 to propose a peace treaty on condition that there would be no further missionizing. This delegation was led by the kikmongwi of Orayvi, one Francisco de Espeleta, who had been baptized and taught to read and write Spanish even before 1680. Immediately prior to this trip, Espeleta had led a force of Orayvis and men from other villages in an attack on Awat'ovi. The village was destroyed, all men who resisted were killed, and the women and children were distributed among the other villages.

With the destruction of Awat'ovi the pro-Christian faction was decisively defeated and the Hopis were able to unite in resisting further missionizing. A year later, in 1701, the Spaniards found they did not have the strength to attack the villages that had been moved to the mesa tops; in 1702, the Hopis tried unsuccessfully to enlist the Zunis in a revolt against the missionaries. Then, in 1706, the Hopis attacked Christian Zunis. The Zunis, however, did not join with them but instead allied themselves with a Spanish retaliatory force which attacked Payupki. The attack failed and for the next 10 years Spanish efforts to persuade the Hopis to cooperate were equally unsuccessful. In 1716 a military expedition was sent to force the Tano Pueblos who had settled the village of Haano on First Mesa to return to the Rio Grande. This effort, like a peaceful invitation in 1718, was unsuccessful.

The refugees had arrived in Hopi country after a period of improved weather conditions had already begun to worsen. A drought lasting from 1727 to 1737 intensified conflicts, presumably over rights to land, among the villages on First Mesa and probably explains the willingness of many of the refugees to return to the Rio Grande during the 1740s (Hackett 1937:472). There is also evidence of a factional split at Orayvi in 1740, "a grave discord over the election of a chief in Oraibe. On this account the pueblo was divided into two parties, who took arms against one another" (Escalante quoted in Thomas 1932:159).

The Hopi population must have reached its peak at about this time. Some estimates (Spicer 1962:195) have placed it in the neighborhood of 8,000, though given the size of the villages this seems excessive. In 1742, 441 Tiwas and other refugees left Payupki and went to live at Isleta, and in 1748 another 350 Tiwas went to settle at Sandia. These returnees, along with the Tanos who remained at Haano on First Mesa, may have swelled the Hopi population to somewhere between 4,000 and 5,000 at the most.

Although the climate began to improve after 1750, a decade of dry years from 1770 to 1779 culminated in a severe drought which forced many Hopis to go to Zuni and Sandia. In 1780, Father Garcia took 200 Hopis and distributed them among the Rio Grande villages. Governor Anza found many Hopis living among the Havasupai and took another 150 Hopis with him to the Rio Grande. Finally, in 1781, a smallpox epidemic hit the Hopis, but the drought was finally broken and crops were good again. By the next year, the Hopis were reported to be in better shape than the Rio Grande Pueblos.

The Hopis were relatively undisturbed by the Spaniards for the remainder of the century. Exactly when Ute and Navajo raiding became a problem is not known, but in 1780 the kikmongwi of Orayvi complained of "continuous war made upon them by the Utes and Navajos" (Thomas 1932:28). Certainly by 1812 at the latest, Navajos began to harass them, and in 1818 Hopis petitioned the government in Santa Fe for help. Raids by Utes and Navajos continued throughout the period of nominal Mexican rule from 1821 to 1846, and increased significantly thereafter. Navajo encroachment made it dangerous for Hopis to farm lands at some distance from the village and thus placed constraints on their ability to cope with conditions of drought.

Whether or not the introduction of Christianity was a bone of contention at Orayvi in 1740 is not known; it is worth noting, however, that the dispute was in the open immediately after a decade of drought. In 1775, Escalante attempted missionary activity at First Mesa. His observations suggest a situation described by Dozier for the Rio Grande

Pueblos: "I found, as in other Pueblos, some rebellious and others intimidated, although the malicious faction is everywhere larger and more numerous" (quoted in Whiteley 1988:25; Adams 1963:130). Does the existence of pro- and anti-Christian sentiment among the Hopi indicate that there were disaffected Hopis who saw in contact with the Spaniards some alternative to their unsatisfactory lives? If so, what was unsatisfactory? Or were there differences of opinion concerning the best way to cope with the Spanish presence? It was Espeleta, after all, who led the antimissionary group that proposed the peace treaty in Santa Fe and who led the attack on Awat'ovi. Yet Espeleta was a kikmongwi who had been educated by the missionaries and converted, at least nominally, to Christianity.

Two patterns of coping with foreign intrusions emerged very clearly during the Spanish period and persisted well into the twentieth century. The first was the Hopi style of diplomacy, which was deceptively conciliatory when the Spaniards appeared strong but invariably hostile when the Hopis did not fear retaliation. After providing several examples, Whiteley (1988:29) concludes that "the Oraibis repeatedly led Spanish representatives to believe they were on the very brink of capitulating, but always actually maintained complete cultural sovereignty" (see also Whiteley 1988:20, 22, 24–26).

The second pattern is that the villages most exposed to contact were the most conciliatory and were the first to accept innovation. Active resistance consistently came from Orayvi, the most distant village, while Awat'ovi accepted missionaries and the villages of First Mesa offered no armed resistance after their initial encounters. These coping strategies must be kept in mind when interpreting the utterances of village chiefs in the late nineteenth and early twentieth centuries.

THE AMERICAN PERIOD TO THE SPLIT OF 1906

The second half of the nineteenth century was marked by accelerated contacts and pressures from the Americans, debilitating epidemics, droughts, and Navajo usurpation of Hopi land.[2] It was on this complex of stresses that the factional split which finally destroyed Orayvi fed and grew. Severe smallpox epidemics hit the villages in 1853, 1866, and 1898. These epidemics seem to have occurred at about the same time as serious droughts. One drought followed hard upon the epidemic of 1853; another began about two years before the epidemic of 1866 and lasted until 1868. There were partial harvest failures in 1899 and 1900; 1902 was the worst year. After 1903 conditions were moister, but the springs at Orayvi failed badly in 1906, the year of the actual splitting of the village. Lines of women waited for hours at the springs to fill their jars with water.

From 1890 on, Hopi agents increasingly complained about Navajo incursions onto the Hopi reservation, which had been established in 1882. By 1900, Navajos were taking over some key watering sites, at a time when the Hopis were being plagued by drought (Whiteley 1988:101). Federal government attempts to allot Hopi lands were followed by missionary activities. An education program attempted to force Hopi children to school at Keams Canyon and, later, to day schools at each of the mesas; it met with angry resistance, which colored relations with the government until after the Second World War.

Initial contacts with the Anglo-Americans had been friendly. A delegation of Hopis went to Santa Fe in 1850 to discuss Navajo depredations and were reassured that the United States was making efforts to control them. By the time an Indian agency of the Bureau of Indian Affairs was set up at Keams Canyon in 1870, there was widespread favorable feeling among the Hopis toward the Americans. Anglo-Americans were viewed as the elder brother, the Pahaana who, according to tradition, was to come out of the East and help the Hopis. That United States troops restrained the Utes and Navajos also contributed to this favorable attitude (Spicer 1962:201). The subsequent education policies of the government and the activities of the various missionaries initiated an ongoing debate among the Hopis over whether or not the Americans were the true Pahaana. There is no evidence to suggest, however, that the leaders of the Friendly faction in Orayvi, or those of other villages, ever based their actions on the belief that the Americans were the Pahaana.

For the most part, however, the village of Orayvi appears to have had an unfriendly attitude toward the Americans even before 1870. The reception of a new agent in 1871 had been cordial in all the villages except Orayvi, where he was told the villagers wanted nothing to do with the government. It also seems that the Orayvi chief was angry with the chiefs of the other Hopi villages because they had adopted a conciliatory posture toward the Americans (Whiteley 1988:40).

The first recorded evidence of the factions at Orayvi is from Frank Cushing, who visited the village in 1882. Loololma, the Bear clan kikmongwi of Orayvi, complained to Cushing that he was being opposed by a group of "witches" (Whiteley 1988:72). At this meeting, Loololma named his principal antagonists and blamed them for "keeping his people poor" and for refusing government annuities. One man is referred to as Loololma's "would be successor," which suggests a dispute over the legitimacy of Loololma's leadership. As all but one of the Orayvi families refused annuities (Whiteley 1988:40), Loololma cannot be said to have adopted a conciliatory position. It is more likely that his primary purpose was to make allies of the Americans.

In 1883, the Hopi agency was relocated from Keams Canyon to the Navajo agency at Fort Defiance, and government influence diminished. Between 1886 and 1889 efforts to get Hopi children into school were initiated. A petition for a school at Keams Canyon was signed by 20 Hopi leaders, most of whom were from First Mesa and none from Orayvi. The boarding school at Keams Canyon was opened in 1887, but the Orayvis refused to send their children there. Loololma sought to delay the inevitable crackdown by making conciliatory statements, promising to send two of his own children and to secure the attendance of several others (Whiteley 1988:74). This tactic was repeated in 1889, when Loololma again promised to send half a dozen children to the government school. Loololma and other Hopi leaders went to Washington in 1890, where they agreed to accept the schools, Christian missionaries, and land allotments as specified by the Dawes Severalty Act of 1887. When school opened, however, Orayvi children were conspicuously absent; total enrollment varied from 2 to 18 during the first two weeks of the school term. The government then threatened to use force, but still no children came. Loololma blamed his enemies for this lack of cooperation, despite the fact that he had not sent his own children. Some leaders of the opposition were arrested, and for several days Loololma sent a few children to the school. Finally, troops were sent to Orayvi, where all the residents behaved in a friendly manner and turned over their children.

Up to this time, Loololma cannot be said to have supported the education program. Rather, he appears to have been trying to postpone the inevitable confrontation by making promises he hoped he would never have to keep. In the past, and on the other mesas, resistance always collapsed once the leaders became convinced that overwhelming punitive actions would be taken against them. Beginning in 1891, however, the leaders of the Hostile faction adopted a belligerent and intransigent posture they were to sustain for over twenty years. In that year, allotment surveyors arrived. Even the First Mesa chiefs were disturbed by what they saw as a move to dispossess them of their land and to destroy the traditional system of landholding. It was at Orayvi, however, that the survey stakes were pulled out each night. Opposition to the school also increased, and when troops were called in they were driven off by about 50 Hostiles. Although the Anglos were ignorant of the fact, this was a formal declaration of war, described in some detail by Titiev (1944:76–77). The Hostile faction was also considering assassinating Loololma before the troops arrived, but the man assigned the job lacked the determination to carry it out. Some nine weeks later, in July, the troops returned in force with Hotchkiss guns. This time they met no resistance, and nine Hostile leaders were arrested.

Despite the Anglos' belief that Loololma supported government policies, there were still no Orayvi children in school in 1892. In the same year, the first "successful" government census of Hopi was completed. Of 853 Orayvis counted, 299 (35 percent) were said to be Hostile. When the day school was opened the following year, only 30 children were in attendance—all of them children of leading Friendly families. The turmoil increased in August 1893, when an aggressive and persistent Mennonite missionary, Henry R. Voth, arrived in Orayvi. This added evidence that the government sought to destroy the Hopi way of life only increased the turmoil. The Hostiles attempted to lay claim to farmlands at Munqapi and also threatened to drive the Friendlies out of Orayvi that spring, so troops were sent in and 19 members of the Hostile faction were arrested and sent to Alcatraz until September 1895. At some point after this, Loololma began to "seed" Munqapi with families loyal to him in order to prevent a Hostile takeover of the well-watered land.

At about this time, Lomahongiwma, head of the Spider clan, proclaimed that he was the true kikmongwi of Orayvi and inaugurated a rival set of ceremonies. There was still great opposition to the school, where enrollment remained at about 30, and to a vaccination program initiated during the smallpox epidemic of 1898.

Loololma died around 1904 and was succeeded by Tawakwaptiwa, the youngest of his sister's sons. The following year, although there had been plenty of snow and rainfall, land again became the subject of dispute. We know little about the nature of the problem, but the agent was called in as a mediator and announced that he would call a council in the winter to decide on a division that would last "till the shifting sands or the receding of the wash makes another division necessary" (Whiteley 1988:101). In the same year, 1905, Yukiwma, the head of Kookop clan, rejected the leadership of Spider clan and successfully replaced Lomahongiwma as the leader of the Hostile faction.

From this moment on, the situation at Orayvi deteriorated rapidly. Early in 1906, a group of Bluebird clansmen were brought in from Second Mesa and assigned some of Bear clan land by the Hostile faction, and an attempt to evict the newcomers was put into effect. After a pushing contest, the Hostiles left the village and established a settlement at Hotvela. Despite government intervention and the arrest of the leaders of both factions, the Hostiles were not allowed to return to Orayvi. In November, troops surrounded the Hotvela settlement, seized 80 children, and took them to the Keams Canyon school. The next week the Hostiles were told that those willing to send their children to school could return to Orayvi. About 25 Hostiles, the followers of the deposed head of Spider clan, Lomahongiwma, accepted. They remained in Orayvi until 1909, when Tawakwaptiwa returned from his imprisonment and evicted them once again; they established the new village of Paaqavi.

Soon after the split of Orayvi, then, several villages existed where before there had been only one. In 1905, Orayvi had a population of about 790, and Munqapi a population of about 85. After the split, Hotvela had a population of around 300, Paaqavi some 130, and Orayvi had declined to about half its former size. In the years that followed, a steady flow of migrants to Munqapi and the new village of Kiqötsmovi (New Orayvi) at the base of Third Mesa depleted the population of Orayvi until, in 1933, there were only 112 people left in what was once the largest of the Hopi villages.

From this review of major events it is possible to reject the notion that opposition to American policies alone led to the creation of factions. Titiev places Loololma's adoption of a pro-American attitude before Cushing's report of the existence of factions in 1882:

> Lololoma's conversion to Americanism occurred early in the Eighteen Eighties. . . . To discuss ways and means of stopping the Navajo, a party of Hopi chiefs was taken to Washington by Thomas Keam. . . . Lololoma was a member of Keam's group and took part in a conference with the President of the United States [probably President Arthur, who was in office from 1881 to 1885]. . . . The trip to Washington made so deep and so favorable impression on Lololoma that it caused him to reverse completely his former attitude towards Americans and their culture. . . . Lololoma's change of policy immediately caused a violent reaction among his people. Some of them favored the new attitude, but a large part of Oraibi's populace was ultra-conservative and vigorously condemned the Village chief's change of heart. (Titiev 1944:72–73)

Loololma's trip to Washington could not have been earlier than 1890. Whiteley (1988:72) searched the archival records without success in an attempt to verify a date in the 1880s. Instead, he found a letter written in 1890 by Thomas Keam, the trader who is said to have taken the Hopi delegation to Washington, stating that none of the Hopis had ever been east of Albuquerque, New Mexico. "Cushing's account of 1882 describes a serious rift almost eight years before Loololma's visit to Washington and five years before the education program affected Oraibi at all" (Whiteley 1988:253).

Nevertheless, Loololma did seek American support against his enemies in 1882. "He [Loololma] talked to me, cried, and begged that I ask Washington for soldiers to help get rid of the witches. He told me they were the ones who opposed the acceptance of annuities, and caused all the troubles in Oraibi, keeping his people poor" (Cushing 1922:267). But, as we have already noted, Loololma did not support the effort to place Hopi children in school when the boarding school at Keams Canyon was opened in 1887. He did, however, attempt to deflect government pressure by making conciliatory statements. In my opinion, Loololma was practicing the type of diplomacy used by the Hopis since Spanish times.

In sum, there is no evidence of any division of opinion concerning Anglo-Americans or their policies prior to the school issue, and even then Loololma did not favor schooling but tried to stall the government with vague promises. The education issue was, as Titiev claimed, a casus belli. Even contemporary observers doubted that the issue was at the heart of the division:

> It is believed by not a few persons who know these Indians well, that their division grew wholly out of the internal political dissentions of the tribe; that one of the factions conceived the device of declaring itself friendly to the United States Government, not because it felt so especially, but because it believed that by such a declaration it could win the favor of the Government and obtain an invincible ally in its struggle with the other faction. . . . I, for one, cherish no illusions as to the meaning of the professions of good will on the part of the friendly faction. (Leupp 1906:124)

Of the proffered explanations of the split, there remain those advanced by Titiev, Bradfield, and Whiteley. Titiev and Bradfield, it will be recalled, have proposed that a restricted land base and a growing population, in conjunction with the fragility of the social structure, made the fissioning of the village inevitable. In the next two chapters, we will test this explanation and Whiteley's notion of a collusion of the leadership of both factions.

CHAPTER 6

Land, Population,
and Social Organization

TITIEV'S ACCOUNT OF THE ORAYVI SPLIT implicates disputes over land
and the inherent fragility of a social system that pits clan ties against
allegiance to the village (Titiev 1944:69, 92–93). Bradfield attempts to
explain these disputes by claiming that Orayvi's fields were being destroyed by erosion at the same time that the population was growing
and exceeding the carrying capacity of the land (Bradfield 1971:29–30).
The fragility of the social system cannot be a *cause* of dissention, however; rather it is an indication of the lines along which the split ought to
take place. That is, some clans should be Friendlies, others Hostiles.
Both authors go on to suggest a deteriorating economy as the root cause
of land disputes. There are problems, however, with each of these
views.

If Titiev is correct about Hopi social organization, the split ought
to have proceeded along clan lines. Yet Titiev himself states that households appear to have moved as units. This was because "the men of the
conflicting clans brought into their respective parties their wives and
children, thus emphasizing household ties and beginning to break up
clan cohesion" (Titiev 1944:92). If this is so, however, one cannot demonstrate that the "fragility" of the social organization had anything to
do with the split. Moreover, the idea that the men influenced their
wives appears unlikely. We have already seen that women of high rank

married men of lesser rank more often than not. If a woman belonging to a prime lineage in a high-ranking clan were a Friendly, is it likely that her low-ranking husband, if a Hostile, could persuade her to abandon her lineage's ceremonial responsibilities and claims to good land? Unless there is evidence of cleavage along clan or lineage lines, or both, this aspect of Titiev's hypothesis must be rejected out of hand.

Bradfield's claim that the main floodplain in the Orayvi valley had been eroded before 1906 is incorrect, as he himself discovered after his work had been completed (Bradfield 1971:45). This is important because Bradfield argues that Bear clan lands had become worthless, leading Spider clan, with viable fields on a tributary watercourse, to claim that Bear clan could no longer perform its ceremonial function, presumably because it had no fields to allocate to Soyal officers. Nevertheless, argues Bradfield,

> The climatic sequence of the later nineteenth century was, I still hold, the ultimate cause of the splitting of the village in 1906. By 1891 the old pueblo had reached the limit of its field resources; the thirteen lean years from 1892 to 1904, by reducing the yield from the cultivated land, put an increasing economic strain on its inhabitants; this strain was reflected in the dissentions which rent the community during those years and which led directly to the schism of 1906. (Bradfield 1971:45)

But how to demonstrate that the limit of the field resources had been reached? We have seen that there was acreage enough in the valley to accommodate a population of 1,000, a number not exceeded at Orayvi during the latter half of the nineteenth century. Moreover, the fact that the factions were well established before 1892 demands that evidence of economic deterioration, restriction of the land base, and even over-population should be demonstrably present prior to 1880.

SOCIAL ORGANIZATION

Let us look first at the lines of cleavage at the time of the split. Factional affiliation may be measured by examining the population at around 1900 and by determining who actually left the village at the time of split. This latter measure would exclude persons who had died before the split and focus on the final affiliations of the participants.

Titiev (1944:87) presents the factional allegiances in 1906 by sex and clan.[1] Of a total of 622 individuals, 52 percent were Friendly. I counted 488 adults 18 years of age and above in 1900 (including those in the census already deceased), 51 percent of whom were Friendly (table 6.1). The cleavage did not go along clan lines. There is, however, a strong indication that economic factors were at work. Members of high- and middle-rank clans were Friendly and those of low-rank clans were Hostile significantly more often than would be expected by chance (table 6.2).

Loololma was able to retain the allegiance of many low- and middle-rank clansmen by settling them at Munqapi, where there was good land and water. There were significantly more women of low-ranking clans in Munqapi and among the Hostiles in Hotvela and Paaqavi than would have happened by chance. Conversely, there were more high-rank women in Orayvi (table 6.3). Low-rank men were Hostile more than expected, but they did not go to Munqapi in greater than expected numbers. Low-rank men were also underrepresented in Orayvi. Instead of a cleavage along clan lines, the splitting of the village looks more like a flight of the landless. Eighty percent of members of low-rank clans of both sexes left Orayvi either for Munqapi or Hotvela, as opposed to 43 percent of the members of high- and 59 percent of middle-rank clans.

The strong association between clan-controlled land and factional allegiance may be seen more easily by using the clan as a unit of measurement and performing a simple regression analysis of the quality of the land controlled against the proportion of adults of each sex remaining loyal to the Village chief (figs. 5, 6). Clans with a total population of less than 15 were omitted from the analysis to control for the vagaries of choices by individuals in clans with only a very few adults. Bear and Spider clans were also excluded, as they were the leaders of the factions and, presumably, political loyalties precluded much individual choice. For both women and men the association was significant; the better the quality of land controlled, the greater the proportion of the clan's population that remained Friendly.

These findings support the contention that the split was a consequence of the degradation of the land, but say nothing about the

TABLE 6.1

FRIENDLIES AND HOSTILES (INCLUDING THOSE DECEASED BEFORE 1906)

	Women			Men		
Clan	Friendly	Hostile	Total	Friendly	Hostile	Total
Bear	5	2	7	7	0	7
Spider	0	4	4	0	7	7
Katsin	3	0	3	2	2	4
Parrot	4	5	9	6	4	10
Rabbit	13	6	19	12	4	16
Snake	1	0	1	2	3	5
Lizard	9	8	17	9	9	18
Sand	3	16	19	4	12	16
Reed	6	13	19	1	9	10
Greasewood	8	10	18	11	8	19
Bow	6	1	7	3	1	4
Maasaw	12	0	12	8	1	9
Kookop	0	3	3	0	9	9
Coyote	12	4	16	13	1	14
Water Coyote	3	11	14	3	7	10
Millet (*leehu*)	0	2	2	0	1	1
Badger	2	6	8	9	10	19
Gray Badger	0	4	4	4	10	14
Navajo Badger	1	0	1	1	2	3
Butterfly	1	0	1	2	1	3
Patki	7	5	12	11	6	17
Piikyas	9	6	15	6	5	11
Rabbitbrush	2	0	2	2	0	2
Squash	0	3	3	1	2	3
Hawk	4	0	4	2	1	3
Crane	1	0	1	3	0	3
Sun	9	5	14	6	2	8
Eagle	1	4	5	1	4	5
Totals	120	118	238	129	121	250
Titiev's Totals[a]	152	134	286	172	164	336

[a]Titiev 1944:87.

TABLE 6.2

CLAN RANK AND FACTION BEFORE 1906

| | Faction | | | | |
| | Friendly | | Hostile | | |
Rank	Obs	(Exp)	Obs	(Exp)	Total
Men[a]					
High	27	(23.22)	18	(21.78)	45
Middle	71	(62.95)	51	(59.05)	122
Low	31	(42.82)	52	(40.17)	83
Totals	129		121		250
Women[b]					
High	22	(19.66)	17	(19.34)	39
Middle	66	(57.98)	49	(57.02)	115
Low	32	(42.35)	52	(41.65)	84
Totals	120		118		238

[a]Chi-square = 10.146; df = 2; $p < .01$.
[b]Chi-square = 7.9; df = 2; $p = .02$.

TABLE 6.3

CLAN RANK AND VILLAGE AFTER 1906

| | Village | | | | | |
| | Orayvi | | Munqapi | | Hotvela/Paaqavi | |
Rank	Obs	(Exp)	Obs	(Exp)	Obs	(Exp)	Total
Women[a]							
High	12	(7.32)	1	(4.34)	8	(9.35)	21
Middle	30	(25.43)	14	(15.07)	29	(32.5)	73
Low	12	(21.25)	17	(12.59)	32	(27.15)	61
Totals	54		32		69		155
Men[b]							
High	15	(13.46)	6	(5.19)	14	(16.35)	35
Middle	45	(35.0)	12	(13.5)	34	(42.5)	91
Low	10	(21.54)	9	(8.31)	37	(26.15)	56
Totals	70		27		85		182

[a]Chi-square = 13.47; df = 4; $p < .01$.
[b]Chi-square = 16.25; df = 4; $p < .01$.

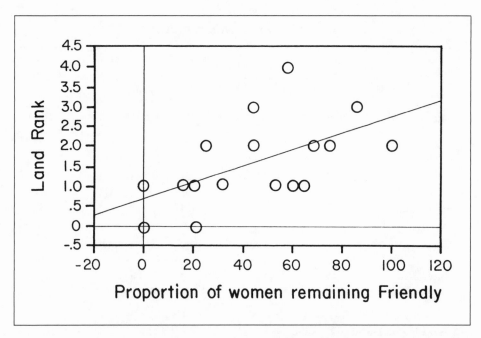

Figure 5. Proportion of women in each clan remaining Friendly, by land rank. ($R^2 = .305$, F test = 6.59; $p = .0215$)

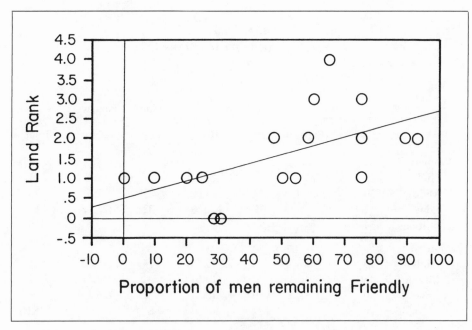

Figure 6. Proportion of men in each clan remaining Friendly, by land rank. ($R^2 = .32$; F test = 7.054; $p = .018$)

fragility of the social system which pitted clan loyalty against village unity. With the exception of Spider and Kookop, the leading clans of the Hostile faction, clans did not act as corporate groups. Crane, Rabbitbrush, and Millet were so small that they must be thought of as moving as lineages or households rather than as clans. By 1906, however, a few clans that had been divided in 1900 had gone over to one faction or the other. Snake clan, which was almost extinct, was entirely Friendly by 1906, as were Katsin, Bow (with the exception of one man), Maasaw, and Hawk clans. But, because some individuals who were minors in 1900 may have retained their parents' allegiances as adults in 1906, these data do not substantially support the idea that the cleavage was along clan lines. Certainly, some clans tended to go more to one side than the other, but the divisions are not clear enough to be significant.

The question then arises if lineage position is a significant factor in determining the way clans split. The prime and alternate lineages of clans with any claim to land might be expected to remain loyal more than the marginal lineages. Since women controlled the land, we may look first at how women of different ranks and lineages aligned themselves. Women of low rank would have little stake in Orayvi lands regardless of lineage, and, in fact, we find that low-rank women of all lineages tended to be Hostile, while prime and alternate lineage women of the middle- and high-rank clans tended to align themselves with the Friendly faction (table 6.4). Again, women of Spider and Bear clans were excluded from analysis because these were the leading clans of the factions. For these women, political pressure would have been more compelling than economic advantage, although the two Bear women who were Hostile were from marginal lineages. Women of the other high-rank clans were most often Friendly if they belonged to prime or alternate lineages. More than clan, then, lineage control of clan lands appears to be an important factor determining response to economic stress and is, moreover, consistent with the importance of the quality of land as a factor in determining factional allegiance.

Lineage position is also important for men, but in a very different way (table 6.5). Low-rank clansmen of prime lineages tended to be Friendly, but lineage was not associated with factional allegiance in either the high- or middle-rank clans due, perhaps, to the fact that the men of these ranks were generally in the Friendly camp. Were the

TABLE 6.4

Lineage	Faction				Total
	Friendly		Hostile		
High-Rank Clans (Bear and Spider Omitted)[a]					
Prime/Alternate	11		3		14
Marginal	4		7		11
Totals	15		10		25
Middle-Rank Clans[b]	Obs	(Exp)	Obs	(Exp)	
Prime/Alternate	26	(20.54)	8	(13.46)	34
Marginal	32	(37.46)	30	(24.54)	62
Totals	58		38		96
Low-Rank Clans[c]					
Prime/Alternate	11	(11.99)	20	(19.01)	31
Marginal	18	(17.01)	26	(26.99)	44
Totals	29		46		75

[a] Fisher's Exact Test $p = .035$.
[b] Chi-square $= 5.7$; df $= 1$; $p = .02$.
[c] Chi-square $= .23$; df $= 1$; $p = .6$ (not significant).

low-rank men married to Friendly women of higher status, or were they more involved in ceremonial activities that provided them with compelling alliances? In my opinion, marriage ties were not a key factor. There are several accounts in Titiev's field notes of marriages that broke up because the couple belonged to different factions. We have seen in chapter 4 that only 3 of 45 women divorced men of opposing factions. I believe that politically harmonious marriages had become the rule long before the actual split: There is no positive evidence for Titiev's assertion that household ties eroded clan solidarity to any great extent.

The question of the importance of ceremonial alliances is difficult to answer because men and women often belonged to more than one ceremonial society, making it impossible to know which demanded the greatest allegiance. Moreover, once the factions had developed,

TABLE 6.5

MEN'S ALLEGIANCE AND LINEAGE

	Faction				Total
Lineage	Friendly		Hostile		
High-Rank Clans (Bear and Spider Omitted)[a]					
Prime	3		3		6
Marginal	16		7		23
Totals	19		10		29
Middle-Rank Clans[b]	Obs	(Exp)	Obs	(Exp)	
Prime	26	(22.38)	7	(10.62)	33
Marginal	33	(36.62)	21	(17.38)	54
Totals	59		28		87
Low-Rank Clans[c]					
Prime	9	(5.45)	7	(10.55)	16
Marginal	7	(10.55)	24	(20.45)	31
Totals	16		31		47

[a] Fisher's Exact Test, $p = .2$ (not significant).
[b] Chi-square $= 2.18$; df $= 1$; $p = .1$ (not significant).
[c] Chi-square corrected for continuity $= 3.93$; df $= 1$; $p = .05$.

men withdrew from societies controlled by clans of the opposing faction: "By the mid-1890s, all 'Friendly' members of these societies had withdrawn, so the ritual sodalities themselves became factional nuclei" (Whiteley 1988:71). The Soyal and Gray Flute societies' memberships were almost entirely in the Friendly camp (table 6.6). Soyal was, of course, controlled by Bear, and any Hostile members would have left the society many years before 1900. If Spider ever provided the War chief in Soyal, it had been replaced by Coyote or Badger long before 1900. Despite the turmoil of the Patki-Piikyas conflict which led to the replacement of the Patki officers in Soyal by Piikyas men, the majority of Patki clan remained loyal, presumably because of their large clan landholdings. The membership of the Gray Flute society, controlled by Patki, was almost entirely loyal. By contrast, Blue Flute and Antelope

TABLE 6.6

MEN'S SOCIETY MEMBERSHIP AND ALLEGIANCE

Society (Clan)	Friendly	Hostile
Soyal (Bear)	23	2
Powamuy (Badger/Katsin)	26	25
Momtsit (Spider/Kookop)	26	27
Taw (Parrot)	11	13
Al (Bow)	13	27
Kwan (Maasaw)	12	13
Blue Flute (Spider)	5	18
Gray Flute (Patki)	29	4
Snake (Snake)	12	19
Antelope (Spider)	2	10
Totals	159	158

Note: Chi-square = 55.98; df = 9; p = .0001.

societies controlled by Spider clan were almost entirely Hostile. The remaining societies were divided evenly between the two factions, with the exception of Al society, which was controlled by the Bow clan. Twice as many Al members were Hostile as Friendly. This is not as clear-cut a division as we find in Soyal, Blue Flute, Antelope, and Gray Flute, but it is worthy of notice. Before 1906 the clan mother of Bow clan was in the Hostile camp, and this may have been a factor.

Because the Friendlies were generally of higher rank than the Hostiles, men of the Friendly faction were also more likely to hold ceremonial office than were men of the Hostiles (table 6.7). The women's societies do not show any tendency to split along factional lines. Larger proportions of Friendly women held ceremonial office and joined societies due to their generally higher status. Sixty percent of the membership in the women's societies and 65 percent of women officeholders were Friendlies.[2]

If the general tendency for the factions to form along "class" lines is clear, it raises questions about those members of prime and alternate lineages of high-rank clans who joined the Hostiles. Is it here we find the influence of marriage ties and ceremonial affiliations? The one mar-

TABLE 6.7
MEN'S CEREMONIAL OFFICES AND ALLEGIANCE

| | Number of Ceremonial Offices | | | | |
| | None | | 1 or More | | |
Faction	Obs	(Exp)	Obs	(Exp)	Total
Friendly	91	(102.7)	40	(28.3)	131
Hostile	105	(93.3)	14	(25.7)	119
Totals	196		54		250

Note: Chi-square = 12.964; df = 1; $p < .001$.

ginal lineage of Bear clan was also Hostile and, considering the small-ness of the clan and its preeminent status, it is important to see if the reasons for its defection can be discovered.

The Bear clan in 1900 was composed of people descended from three sisters, two of whom had died by 1900 (fig. 7). Tuvewunqa's two daughters, Kuwanhongqa and Talashongsi, were Hostiles. Her two sons were Friendlies. This was the alternate lineage before Tuvewunqa died, but a marginal one by 1900. Tawanömqa's oldest daughter, Humiwunsi, became clan mother, but she also died, and because she had no daughters, the position went to her younger sister, Pongyanömsi. Unfortunately, Pongyanömsi was childless, as was her aunt, Nasiletsnöm, and so Humiwunsi's son, Tawakwaptiwa, became Village chief after Loololma's death. Tuvewunqa's first husband was a Hostile; her second a Maasaw clansman whose factional affiliation is not known. He died, and Tuvewunqa married a Lizard clansman who was a Friendly. Tuvewunqa died before 1900, but both her daughters went to Hotvela and then to Paaqavi.

This is not an example of household or lineage unity, since Tuvewunqa's sons and third husband were Friendlies. Tuvewunqa's daughter, Kuwanhongqa, believed that she should have been made clan mother: she "felt herself to be mother of all in the village" (Titiev n.d.). Was this the reason for her to be Hostile? To answer this we would have to know when and why she became alienated from Loololma.

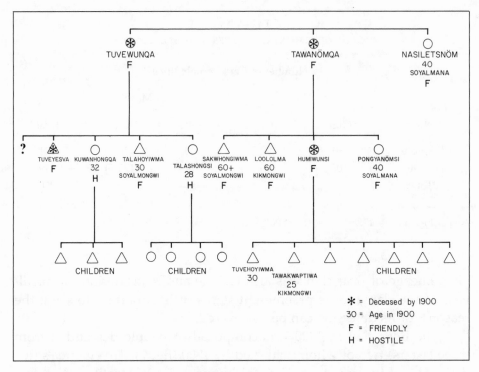

Figure 7. Bear clan.

Tawakwaptiwa told Titiev that Loololma had been training Tuvewunqa's son, Talahoyiwma, to become kikmongwi and that he had been acting as Soyalmongwi for three years but had died (it was thought to have been suicide) before Loololma. With the data available one can only say that neither ceremonial ties nor marital allegiance played a role in the matter. That two women in the prime and alternate lineages were childless in succeeding generations may have confirmed Tuvewunqa's daughters' belief that they should have succeeded to the leadership of the clan during a period when the legitimacy of Bear clan's ability to lead was in question.

The Bow clan defections are also interesting when we recall that Bow was also a clan of high rank. A version of the myth told by Loololma to Tawakwaptiwa says that Bow and Spider clans were partners in mischief, causing so much trouble in the underworld that Matsito, the Bear clan chief, decided to order an emergence (Titiev 1944:73). The telling is clearly an attempt to cast the blame for all troubles on the

Hostiles. It departs from general Hopi tradition, which tells of the dissolution of the people and the chiefs planning the emergence.[3] The clan mother, Talasvenqa, was 60 years old in 1900 but died by 1906. She was Hostile, as was her son, Qötsventiwa, who was Al chief (fig. 8). Her husband was also Hostile and had died before 1900. He was a member of the Antelope society, so it is possible that his low status and ceremonial affiliation were the reasons he became a Hostile and, in the absence of any other evidence, it is possible that Talasvenqa followed her husband. Qötsventiwa was Al chief, at least for a while, and was also in the Antelope society, which may have influenced his politics.[4]

At some point, the sons of Qöyahongnöm held the position of Al chief, but the relationship between Talasvenqa and Qöyahongnöm is not clear. Kennard's genealogy lists them as sisters, and the 1900 census lists both as being about 60 years old. Titiev, on the other hand, says that Talasvenqa was the "real" grandmother of the two sons of Qöyahongnöm. In any event, Qöyahongnöm's older son became Al chief but went insane and died, after which the position passed to his younger brother who also went insane and died. This family was Friendly, as

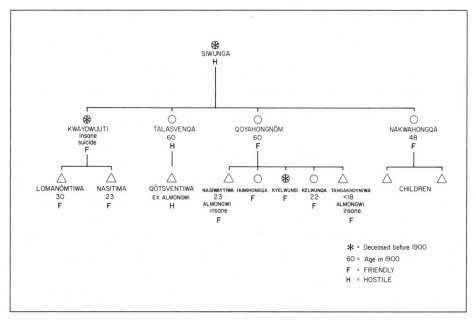

Figure 8. Bow clan.

was that of another sister, Nakwahongqa. The oldest sister, Kwayow-uuti, also a Friendly, is also said to have been insane. She decided to go to Munqapi but committed suicide by jumping into Coal Canyon on the journey there.

Despite the fact that the women of the prime lineage returned to the Friendly faction, I believe that the insanity in the clan was taken by other Orayvis as some sort of divine punishment for the original defection of the prime lineage of this important clan. It may also be the reason Loololma projected the evil quality of the clan back into the mythical past. A daughter of Qöyahongnöm, Humihongqa, married twice, both times to Navajos—which would also have been considered deviant.

The prime and alternate lineage of the Parrot clan also split. All of the Crows who were calling themselves Parrots (marginal lineages) were Hostile, with the exception of one young woman who was married into a family with positions in Soyal. The prime lineage—the clan mother and her oldest daughter—remained loyal. The younger sisters were Hostile, as were the two brothers. One of the Parrot men was in Antelope society, as was the second husband of one of the Hostile sisters. Other than this, there is no indication of the reason for this defection. One Patki man in the prime lineage was also a Hostile and was a member of the Antelope society. There would appear then to be a variety of reasons for individuals to have made the choice to join the Hostiles other than economic interest. These reasons, however, were diverse and do not obscure the economic factor.

POPULATION AND CARRYING CAPACITY OF THE LAND

Bradfield's argument that Orayvi's population was growing at the same time the quality of the land was deteriorating has been questioned by Whiteley (1988:247–51), who raises several objections: (1) that leadership was based on control over ritual knowledge and not over land, "the 'supposed' economic ground of their leadership was thus not susceptible to undermining"; (2) that there were many alternative lands available, especially at Munqapi, "which was increasingly absorbing elements of Oraibi's population," and that these areas comprised "readily available alternatives that were in fact being used"; and (3) that the availability of wage work and access to commodities at the Orayvi store "provided palpable supplements to the subsistence economy by the late 1890s."

With the exception of the claim that Hopi leadership was not based on control of land, an issue already dealt with, each of these points demands consideration. Whiteley himself provides some indication of what these considerations might be. His informants mentioned population pressure as one of the elements in the split, as well as the failure of Orayvi's water supply. Elsewhere, a Navajo encroachment on Hopi land, another factor limiting the availability of alternative field sites, is mentioned:

> Many Navajos from the Navajo Reservation have settled along the water courses and at the watering places on Moqui land. Why this has been allowed I cannot understand, as the Navajo Reservation is the largest in the United States and the Moqui Reservation is comparatively small. These places taken by the Navajos are the very best ones on the reservation and control most of the water supply. (Agent Burton, 1899, quoted in Whiteley 1988:102)

"During the years of drought, especially, the Navajo presence must have been particularly threatening," remarks Whiteley (1988:102). Whiteley's primary objection to Bradfield's position, it seems to me, is for the most part a reaction against an argument he believes implicitly represents the split "as a reflex response to economic conditions that surpassed the Oraibi's leaders' grasp . . . a behaviorist implication that the mindless Hopis, uncomprehending the conditions of their existence, responded like laboratory rats to randomly changed stimuli" (Whiteley 1988:251). Without debating the issue of whether a behaviorist explanation ipso facto denies human intelligence and choice, we may leave Hopi perceptions and actions to be dealt with in the final chapter and turn our attention to the issues of carrying capacity and excess population.

Looking at population change and environmental stress over long periods of time, there is ample evidence that Hopis left their villages for varying periods of time during prolonged and serious droughts. Hopi families kept two or three years' supply of corn in reserve for those years when crops failed. More serious droughts forced families with the most drought-prone lands to seek farming sites at some distance from the village. During short-lived droughts a family could sometimes survive by farming several distant fields. If the drought affected most of the region, however, people were often forced to seek refuge among other tribes.

The droughts that affected the Hopis between 1867 and 1900 involved a degradation of the water tables as serious as that of the period between A.D. 1200 and 1300, when the Hopis abandoned Black Mesa and surrounding areas and settled at the southern edge of the mesa where they live today. The erosion of the Jeddito Wash continued until Antelope Mesa sites—with the exception of Awat'ovi—were completely abandoned by the time of the Spanish entradas. Spanish estimates of the Hopi population were often unreliable. In 1583, for example, Espejo said there were 50,000 Hopis, while Luxan reported 12,000 (McIntire 1970). Estimates of 3,000 in 1614 and 2,966 in 1664 appear more reasonable, if only because they are in agreement (McIntire 1970; Spicer 1962:190). Archaeological evidence points to sporadic occupation of Canyon de Chelly by small groups of Hopis from the fourteenth to the nineteenth century, but especially prior to 1700 (Steen 1966:55–57).

The environment deteriorated again between about 1690 and 1770. Although this period of stress was not as severe as the earlier one, it did cause many former refugees to return to the Rio Grande. In the mid-1700s, many Hopi families also left their villages due to drought and famine and took refuge among the Navajos, particularly in Canyon de Chelly. In one instance involving 40 families, the Hopi men were killed and the women and children taken in (Grant 1978:82). That Hopis also went to live with the Havasupai and with other Pueblos has already been mentioned. Just how large the Hopi population was before the refugees left we don't know, but it may have grown to something near 4,500. Almost 1,000 Tewa refugees returned to the Rio Grande area, leaving only the village of Haano behind.

The droughts of the late 1770s were followed by a smallpox epidemic in 1781 which further reduced the population. Figure 9 correlates population with average water table levels for the region. Without arguing about absolute numbers for these early periods, we see that population and environment co-vary. Population increases that might

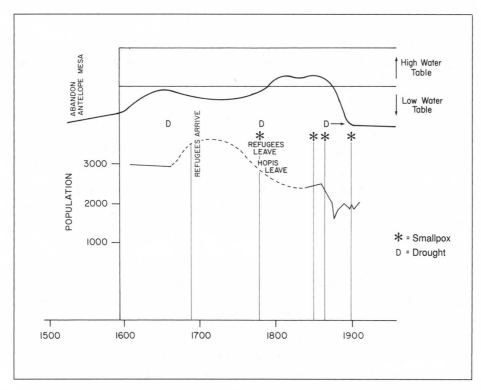

Figure 9. Tribal population and water tables.

have been expected in the nineteenth century were attenuated by the smallpox epidemics, and the population did not reach 3,000 again until well into the twentieth century. Although we cannot know the carrying capacities of the lands farmed by each of the three mesa villages, it is clear that during serious droughts, varying numbers of Hopis were forced to leave until conditions improved.

The village of Munqapi some 40 miles west of Orayvi and, perhaps, Cow Springs Wash some 40 miles to the north were well-watered areas farmed by the Orayvis. There are no historical accounts of Hopi use of Cow Springs Wash until the twentieth century, but Hopi farming in the Munqapi area has a long history. The question is if and when it served as an adequate alternative for Orayvi families during times of severe drought.

During the latter half of the seventeenth century, Munqapi was occupied by Yuman speakers, certainly Havasupais (Hackett 1937:264).

In 1686 the Havasupais were reported to have been defeated by the Apaches, who were most likely Navajos (Bandelier 1892:383). Then, in 1692, de Vargas reported the "Coninas" living about 25 miles west of the Hopis, which suggests that Havasupai settlement extended as far east as the lower end of Blue Canyon at that time (Forbes 1966:351). In 1775, a "Cosnina" told Escalante that the first ranchitos of his people were about three days travel west of Orayvi (Adams and Chavez 1956: 302), and Havasupais were at war with the Navajos when Spaniards visited Munqapi and Orayvi in 1776 (Coues 1900:356–58, 403). The Havasupais identified a half-ruined pueblo as belonging to the Hopis of Orayvi and said that the Hopis planted some crops there. It is clear that at this time the Hopis used land as far west, and the Havasupais as far east, as Munqapi.

In 1823, Munqapi was called Los Algodones, which means "cotton plants" and is a translation of the old Navajo name for Munqapi. The Havasupais had withdrawn from the area and the Navajos advanced into it between 1776 and 1823; hostilities between Navajos and Havasupais as early as 1776 have been noted. In 1801, a war by Navajos against Hopis and Havasupais was reported (New Mexico State Record Center Archives). Prior to the exile of Navajos to Fort Sumner in 1864, the Munqapi area was used by Hopis, Paiutes, and Navajos. The Hopis used Munqapi as a summer field colony and, due to the frequency of Navajo raiding, the fields were devoted mainly to cotton, which demanded less attention than food crops and which was less likely to be expropriated by Navajos. During the period that most Navajos were at Fort Sumner there were some raids by Anglo "citizens" against Navajos west of the Hopis who had not been rounded up. Reports from the time make no mention of Hopis living west of Orayvi, suggesting that the Navajo presence placed considerable constraints on Hopi use of the land.

The Mormons came to Munqapi and nearby Monavi sometime between 1868 and 1873 (Cleland and Brooks 1955:264–78). The missionary John D. Lee mentions that Tuba (Tuuvi) was the "principal" of the village at this time, and that he was a Walpi chief.[5] While staying at Monavi, Lee visited Munqapi and reported that there were Orayvis, Navajos, and Paiutes farming there. On September 6, 1873, a Hopi named Talti told Lee that all the Hopis at Munqapi had returned to

Orayvi except Talti, his son, Tuuvi, and Tuuvi's wife (Cleland and Brooks 1955:288, 292–94). They asked Lee to settle at Munqapi to prevent trouble from the Navajos who were living close by at Pasture Canyon (Tanner Creek), which joins Munqapi Wash below the village site. Trouble between Mormons and Navajos led Mormons to leave the area until 1875, at which time they built a stone house at Munqapi (McClintock 1921:137, 155–57). To me, this suggests that the Hopis were not able to farm the area without risk and that there was no permanent Hopi population there at that time. By 1879, however, the Hopis complained of Mormon encroachment on Munqapi lands. At this time, the Mormon population was divided between Munqapi and Tuba City and numbered a little over 100.

In June 1888, H. S. Welton (1888), Special Indian Agent, reported a Hopi population at Munqapi of 16: four men, six women, five boys, and one girl. "Since the Mormons have taken nearly all the land and water others who used to come from Oraibi no longer do so. The Indians are permitted to keep some land but are deprived of enough water to irrigate it."[6] Then, in 1894, "in order to safeguard their claim (and possibly at the instigation of Mormon settlers), a group of about fifty Hostiles . . . went to Moencopi and planted the land with wheat" (Whiteley 1988:86). As a counter to this move, Loololma decided to send permanent residents to Munqapi, but exactly when this took place and whether or not the 86 Munqapi residents enumerated by the 1900 census were there on a permanent basis cannot be known with certainty.[7] Troubles with the Navajos continued until the government bought out Mormon claims in 1900. The Mormons vacated Munqapi and Tuba City in 1903.

The fields along Cow Springs Wash were farmed by Munqapi Hopis after the government made Tuba City an agency and moved the school from Blue Canyon to Tuba City in 1904. A Navajo policeman, John Daw of Gallup, had settled near Red Lake, which made the Munqapi Hopis feel more secure. I suspect Orayvis had farmed here on a part-time basis prior to the westward movement of the Navajo population after their release from Fort Sumner. After the split, as more and more Hopis moved to Munqapi, the Cow Springs fields were used fairly intensively until the 1930s, when the area was incorporated into the Navajo reservation and the Hopis were evicted. There were other areas farmed by the Hopis during times of drought, but with the exception of the springs at Paaqavi they are not well identified.

Whiteley also mentions the availability of wage work and store-bought goods serving to ameliorate any economic distress there may have been. Wage-work opportunities were remarkably limited for the Orayvis. A few men were employed by the resident missionary, and it is possible that the Mormons may have provided occasional jobs for the resident population of Munqapi. That a significant proportion of the families in the village could have relied on wage work as an alternative source of subsistence seems doubtful. There was no store in Orayvi until about 1898, and a Hopi opened a second store in 1902 (Whiteley 1988:102–3). Certainly, these stores were established rather late in the history of the Hopi drought. More important is the fact that they did not stock items of much nutritional value. Speaking of 1890, but referring primarily to First Mesa, Fewkes (1922:270–71) reports that "purchases from the store were limited to the simplest staple necessities, as calico, flour, sugar, tobacco, and coffee. . . . Matches, tobacco, yeast cakes, and candy were in great demand." Of even greater importance nutritionally, in my opinion, were the sheep raised by the Hopi or traded for with the Navajos, although whether the Hopis could offer much in trade during severe drought years is doubtful.

These observations on alternative sources of subsistence items do not answer our questions definitively. There were fields north of the clan lands on the Orayvi Wash that Bradfield (1971:21) believes were brought into permanent cultivation after 1850. It is clear that there were farming sites at varying distances from the village. It is also apparent that raiding Navajos made the use of these more distant sites precarious. The question is whether the Navajo presence limited their use to the point that the Orayvi population exceeded the carrying capacity of the land available to it. In this context, it is important to remember that the traditional Hopi response to severe drought was temporary migration of the excess population and not village fissioning. Was there anything different about the sequence of events at Orayvi that made this response impossible or inadequate? Bradfield's claim that Orayvi's population was actually growing during this period would, if verified, suggest that emigration was constrained, or that there was immigration from other mesas.

TABLE 6.8

HOPI POPULATION ESTIMATES

			Population				
Year	Small-pox	Drought	First Mesa	Second Mesa	Third Mesa	Total	Source
1846						2,450	Gov. Charles Bent
1851			1,200	900	650	2,750	Bradfield reconstruction
1852			4,000			8,000	Dr. Ten Broeck
1853	(1853)					2,000	Lt. Whipple
1861			650	1,050	800	2,500	Agt. John Ward
		(1864)					
1865						3,000	Agt. John Ward[a]
	(1866)	(1866)					
1872					600		W. C. Powell[b]
1874						1,950	BIA[a]
1877			568	536	500	1,604	W. H. Jackson
1883						1,800	Dr. Ten Kate Jr.[a]
1890			496	595	905	1,996	U.S. Census
1892					853		Mayhugh[b]
1899	(Severe)					1,832	Agt. Leo Crane[a]
1900			537	537	858	1,932	U.S. Census
1901						1,841	Secretary of the Interior[a]
1904						1,878	BIA[a]
1910						2,009	U.S. Census[a]

Sources: Bradfield (1971:61–63) except where noted.
[a]McIntire 1970.
[b]Whiteley 1988:81.

Population estimates for the total Hopi population after 1846 appear reasonable with the exception of that of Dr. Ten Broeck for 1852, which appears much too high (table 6.8). Bradfield's re-estimation, although it is more in line with other estimates, has the population of Second Mesa higher than that of Third Mesa, which in my opinion may not be warranted. First and Third mesas had fields on the floodplains of their respective washes; Second Mesa did not. The land available to the Second Mesa villages was along tributary watercourses and side valley slopes; that is, medium- and poor-grade land. In addition, the Second Mesa villages did not control all the fields of any of the washes, but used some of the areas on the east side of Orayvi Wash and along a tributary to Wipho Wash controlled by First Mesa. Moreover, Second Mesa had a reputation for resisting immigration from First Mesa (Fred Eggan, personal communication, 1989). I think it quite possible that Third Mesa was larger prior to the smallpox epidemic of 1853 and that it does not show population loss afterward due to immigration from the other mesas, as well as from natural increase. Ward's estimate of the Second Mesa population in 1861 also appears high.

There is no reason to believe that First Mesa took the brunt of the epidemic in 1853 or that Second Mesa was the only population affected in 1866–67. Evidence for one of the mesas escaping the ravages of an epidemic exists only for Orayvi in 1899, when the government created a *cordon sanitaire* between it and the Second Mesa villages (Whiteley 1988:90–91). Variations in mesa populations using Bradfield's estimate for 1850 show increases in Orayvi's population between that time and 1900 (fig. 10). There is no need to argue the merits or demerits of

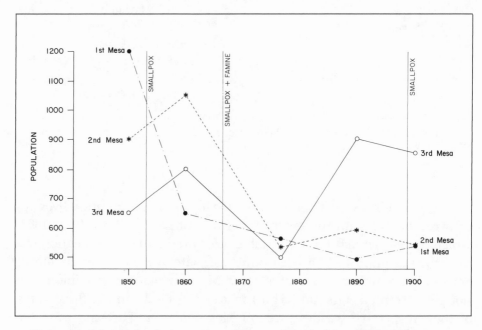

Figure 10. Mesa populations, droughts, and epidemics, 1850–1900.

Bradfield's assumptions; it is more important to examine what happened after the serious drought, famine, and epidemic that covered the sixteen-year period of 1865 to 1880.

The years from 1851 to 1865 had been fairly moist, but in 1866 a long period of drought began. Severe drought and famine between 1866 and 1868 were followed by a smallpox epidemic (Titiev 1944:72). After reviewing historical accounts and tree-ring records, Bradfield (1971:28) concludes that "there was a long period of rain insufficiency from around 1865 through 1904, culminating in a 13 year drought from 1892–1904, and that the drought was broken by a series of great storms early in 1905." These storms, however, came in the form of winter rains; the summer was dry and, as we have seen, the water tables were so low that the spring at Orayvi had gone almost completely dry. The First Mesa floodplains at Polacca and Wipho washes were beginning to erode around 1890, and by 1900 they were destroyed entirely (Forde 1931: 363; Thornthwaite, Sharpe, and Dosch 1942:104–7). This circumstance would have precluded any shift of population from Orayvi to the other mesas after 1892 or so.

Regardless of what the populations were on the three mesas prior to the drought, famine, and smallpox epidemic of 1865–66, they plummeted after that time; in 1877 none exceeded 600. By 1890, though, Orayvi may have had a population of about 900. Aside from these estimates, what is the evidence for population growth at Orayvi? And can immigration be demonstrated or reasonably inferred?

A detailed study of architectural change in Orayvi from 1871 until the 1930s has led Cameron (1990:113–14, 121–23) to the conclusion that between 1871 and 1887 there was a net increase in the total number of rooms of around 10 to 15 percent. Between 1887 and 1901, at least 85 new rooms were built, not counting upper-story rooms in multistory houses. If each household contained between four and six people, the new roomblocks represent an increase of between 140 and 210 people after 1887. Although the total population of Orayvi increased considerably between 1871 and 1901, Cameron finds no evidence of a sudden influx of population, and is of the opinion that natural growth accounted for most of the increase. Bradfield felt that approximately one-third of the increase was due to immigration (Bradfield 1971:62). There would have been an increase in the neighborhood of 30 percent if the population was 600 in 1872 and 858 in 1900. These numbers are consistent with Cameron's estimates and would have exceeded the Navajo population growth for the same period, which was approximately 25 percent.[8] Given the fertility and child survival rates derived from the 1900 census, it is questionable that natural increase alone could account for the increase.

There is some evidence for immigration in Kennard's genealogies. A marginal lineage of Gray Badger clan is noted to have come from First Mesa; the senior generation, consisting of two sisters and a brother, were all Hostiles. Only one woman, Tsorvenqa, was alive in 1900, at which time she was 47 years old. Her sister and brother are said to have been younger. If their parents came to Orayvi the year the oldest was born or when she was an infant, they would have arrived in 1853, the year the smallpox epidemic was said to have been particularly severe on First Mesa.

Two sisters and one brother of a marginal lineage in Patki clan are noted by Kennard as having originated in Songoopavi; all three were said to have been born in Orayvi. In 1900, the oldest was 34 years of age. If the parents had immigrated the year the oldest was born, they would have arrived in 1866, the year Bradfield believed a smallpox epidemic was particularly bad on Second Mesa. Although Patki was a high-rank clan, these children of immigrants were all Hostiles. The lack of definitive evidence notwithstanding, I suspect Bradfield's guess that a third of the population increase between 1853 and 1900 was due to immigration is correct, and that several other immigrant lineages were not identified by Kennard. The Crows who "called themselves Parrots" and some of the several lineages of Rabbit are likely candidates, as all seem to have become extinct "recently" (i.e., within memory of the older informants in 1932) on other mesas (Eggan 1950:65).

In 1900, the populations on each of the mesas were quite different from one another (fig. 11). Those of First and Second Mesa look like other preindustrial populations under stress, with less than half their populations under age 20. By contrast, over half the populations of Third Mesa and of the Navajos living on the Hopi reservation are under age 20 (table 6.9).

As early as 1881 Bourke was struck by the large number of children at Orayvi (Bradfield 1971:62). By a "careful count," there were about

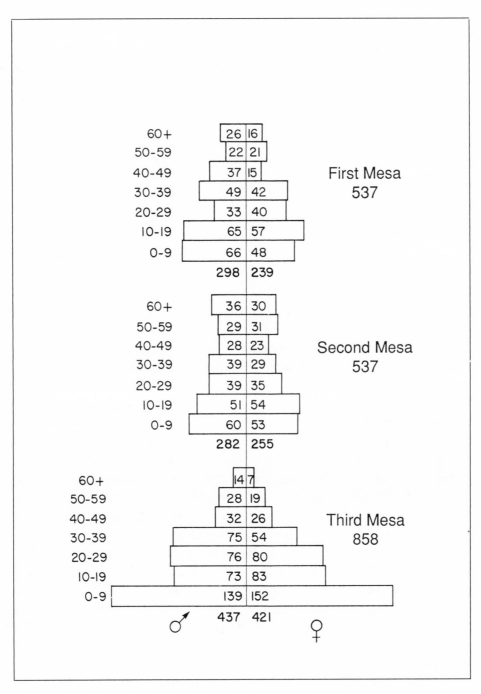

Figure 11. Mesa populations by age and sex, ca. 1900.

TABLE 6.9

INTERMESA COMPARISONS: AGE COHORT AS PERCENTAGE OF
TOTAL POPULATION

Age	First Mesa	Second Mesa	Third Mesa	Navajo[a]
60+	7.8	12.3	2.4	6.8
50–59	8.0	11.2	5.5	4.5
40–49	9.7	9.5	6.7	6.2
30–39	16.9	12.7	15.0	11.1
20–29	13.6	13.8	18.2	14.1
10–19	22.7	19.5	18.2	19.6
0–9	21.2	21.0	33.9	37.7

[a] Includes only Navajos from the Hopi reservation. Source: Johansson and Preston 1978:15.

203 children 8 years of age and younger; these data are in accord with the 291 children between 0 and 9 years of age counted in 1900. The smallpox epidemic of 1899 may have hit the children of the other mesas harder than it did those of Orayvi and thus account for much of this difference, but there are also considerable dissimilarities among mesas in the older age cohorts. This suggests that migration may also account for some of the variability (table 6.10).

Over half of the differences among the mesas are accounted for by the smaller number of people over age 40 on Third Mesa and the greater number of that age cohort on Second Mesa. This information tends to support Bradfield's contention that people left First Mesa for Second Mesa at the time of the first smallpox epidemic in 1853, and that Third Mesa had a smaller population at that time than either of the others. The next important difference is the greater number of individuals between 20 and 29 years of age on Third Mesa—which, I believe, is a product of a higher rate of natural increase on Third Mesa—and the smaller number of people between 30 and 39 years of age on Second Mesa. The Second Mesa numbers are probably due in large part to a migration of younger people from Second to Third Mesa at the time of the 1866 epidemic.

Third Mesa also had higher survival rates of children than the other mesas, as well as fewer childless women and higher fertility (table

TABLE 6.10

INTERMESA COMPARISONS OF AGE COHORTS

Age	First Mesa		Second Mesa		Third Mesa		Total
	Obs	(Exp)	Obs	(Exp)	Obs	(Exp)	
			Adults and Children[a]				
≥20	301	(286.57)	319	(286.57)	411	(457.87)	1,031
≤19	236	(250.43)	218	(250.43)	447	(400.13)	901
Totals	537		537		858		1,932
			Adults 20 + Years of Age[b]				
40 +	137	(128.46)	177	(136.14)	126	(175.4)	440
30–39	91	(84.08)	68	(89.11)	129	(114.81)	288
20–29	73	(88.46)	74	(93.75)	156	(120.79)	303
Totals	301		319		411		1,031

[a]Chi-square = 19.75; df = 2; p = .0001.
[b]Chi-square = 51.19; df = 4; p <.0001.

6.11). These comparisons tempt one to say, with Whiteley, that Third Mesa was really not badly off, with no population pressure and no significant deterioration of its land base. A look at the Navajos living on the Hopi reservation, however, removes this temptation. Although there were more childless women on First Mesa than one would expect by chance, it is really the fact that the Navajos had so few childless women that makes the difference significant (Chi-square = 11.14; df = 3; p <.02). Even Third Mesa had significantly more childless women than the Navajos, when the two groups are considered alone (Chi-square = 4.96; df = 1; p <.05). Conditions were also better for the Navajos, who raised more sheep, lived in less crowded and unsanitary conditions, and were able to move freely in search of farming sites. With fewer children per woman, their children's survival rates were far better than those of the Third Mesa Hopis. Third Mesa, in turn, had better survival rates than the other mesas, but especially better than Second Mesa, which lost many children during the epidemic of 1899.[9]

Taken singly, the issues discussed in this chapter do not demonstrate

TABLE 6.11

FERTILITY AND CHILD SURVIVAL ON THREE MESAS (WOMEN 33+ YEARS)

	Fertility[a] and Child Survival Rates				
	Childless	Bearing	Total	Fertility	% Surviving
First Mesa	9	71	80	6.51	40.7
Second Mesa	8	82	90	7.34	35.2
Third Mesa	3	80	83	8.09	47.5
Navajo[b]	2	129	131	5.3	79.4

	Survival of Children[c]				
	Died		Survived		
	Obs	(Exp)	Obs	(Exp)	Total
First Mesa	274	(271.1)	188	(190.9)	462
Second Mesa	390	(353.2)	212	(248.75)	602
Third Mesa	340	(379.7)	307	(267.3)	647
Totals	1004		707		1711

[a] Fertility given as number of children born per fertile woman.
[b] Source: Johansson and Preston 1978.
[c] Chi-square = 19.4; df = 2; $p < .0001$.

unequivocally that economic distress was the underlying reason for the Orayvi split. Considered together, however, I believe the weight of the evidence does suggest that the population exceeded the capacity of the land to support it during a prolonged period of drought, in part because of the decreased productivity of the land and in part due to the constraints placed upon the use of field areas at some distance from the valley of the Orayvi Wash. That similar fissioning did not occur on the other mesas is primarily due, I think, to the fact that although their lands were distressed, their populations had decreased to the point that each family (at First Mesa at any rate) could choose up to four fields in different areas. On First Mesa, for example, clans owned lands on both Polacca and Wipho washes, so that families could farm several different types of field; this was the situation described by Forde (1931) and modeled by Hegmon (1989). Although there was factional dissention at Second Mesa near the end of the nineteenth century and the disaffected group allied itself with the Orayvi Hostiles, factionalism was never so extreme that one group had to leave the village.

Even if an economic explanation for the split is accepted at this juncture, important questions remain to be answered. If, for example, the revolt was primarily one of landless families, why did Spider clan become a leader of the Hostiles? It owned land of medium quality and, at one time at least, a plot of Bear clan land. Why, if the split had its origins in disputes over land, did the rhetoric of the Hostile faction focus on federal education policy? It is to these and other questions, including Whiteley's argument, that attention will be turned in the next chapter.

CHAPTER 7

Myths, Prophecies, and Political Action

THE EVENTS WE HAVE BEEN DISCUSSING lie far in the past; the individuals involved, their motivations and aspirations, are almost beyond our reach. Historical materials have been written by outsiders and Hopi accounts have been reshaped over time, the tellers having no direct experience of the events. Yet, the abstract analysis presented here leaves us wondering how the momentous events leading up to the disintegration of Orayvi were experienced and interpreted by the Hopis who lived through them. In his book *Deliberate Acts* (1988), Peter Whiteley has presented Hopi interpretations from a variety of sources and times, from what little was recorded by observers at the time to later accounts by Hopis from the 1930s to the present. He concludes his discussion with this synopsis:

> The Hopi analysis of the Oraibi split, which I have offered as that made by the more knowledgeable sector of society, concentrates on a set of features;
>
> 1) The split was a deliberate plot, brought into operation by Oraibi's active *pavansinom*, or politico-religious leaders, via the subtle machinations of Hopi political action.
> 2) The split was foretold in a body of prophecies, recorded in ritual narrative and song, and the years prior to the

split were recognized as fulfilling the conditions set forth in the prophecies as appropriate for the destruction of the village.

3) The split's primary purpose was radical change in the structure of society.
4) Such radical change was directed particularly toward the politico-religious order, which was regarded as the central axis of the social system.

This analysis does not seek for unitary, deterministic causes. Its emphasis on the above features as primary by no means excludes other factors in the split's background, including internal political struggle, population pressure upon waning resources, and powerful acculturative pressure. What distinguishes the Hopi analysis is its emphasis upon the processes of Hopi political and social action within their cultural and historical contexts. A crucial difference between this and the anthropological analyses is the injection of a deliberate, decision-making element with specifiable sociocultural consequences. By contrast, the anthropological analyses, in their various ways, all imply an unwitting reflex response by an unintelligent social organism to uncomprehended forces of change. (Whiteley 1988:283)

The "deliberate acts" in the Hopi interpretations provided are not those of individuals reacting to and attempting to control the changing world about them, but those of ceremonial leaders plotting together to fulfill ancient prophecies which foretold the split. It was also important to do this in such a way that the common people would not suspect the leaders were in collusion but would accept that there were irreconcilable differences of opinion and that the people must choose between them and act accordingly. Whiteley places the "Hopi interpretation" alongside the "anthropological analyses" without further discussion, and the reader is asked only to accept "the proximate idea that the split was a deliberate plan that had as a primary purpose the ending of the ritual order," and "since the ritual order did indeed disintegrate at Third Mesa in a rapid, systematic manner (for the most part), the evidence would seem to corroborate the hypothesis rather well" (Whiteley 1988:290).

This chapter is an attempt to calibrate anthropological analysis with Hopi interpretation in a manner consistent with both. Special attention will be paid to what may have motivated the leading players to act in the ways they did, to determine whether prophecy preceded or followed from the events foretold, and to examine how the precedents set in myth were followed or shaped to contemporary political purposes. This effort must, of necessity, be largely speculative. Events for the most part, especially prior to 1890, are unknown, and the first documentation of the prophecies may not represent their initial pronouncement.

Three prophecies were involved: (1) that the Pahaana, the elder brother of the Hopi, would someday return to help the Hopis in their hour of need; (2) that Spider clan would leave Orayvi and return to Kawestima, a village to the northwest where the clan had lived before coming to Orayvi; (3) that after the split, Orayvi would be destroyed and its ceremonies become extinct.

We have no myths from Third Mesa antedating the development of factions, and those collected at First Mesa by Alexander Stephen in the nineteenth century may not be used as "controls" with any confidence because many First Mesa traditions are quite different from those found on Second and Third mesas. In addition, the myths gathered during the early years of this century from Second Mesa may be influenced by a similar factional division which developed on that mesa. The adequacy of the proposed reconstruction, then, rests on the extent to which it is consonant with Hopi beliefs, on the one hand, and the anthropological analysis, on the other.

We recall that the first documented evidence of factions at Orayvi was provided by Frank Cushing, who visited the village in 1882. At that time, the division already appears to have been deep and the leaders of the Hostiles were clearly identifiable. We have also seen that the federal government's demand that Hopi children attend school had not yet become an issue and that Loololma and other leaders had not yet made their famous visit to Washington. The Hopi Agency had, however, been established at Keams Canyon, and contacts with Anglo-Americans had been frequent during the 1860s. What, then, had triggered the dispute in the years prior to 1880?

According to Hopi tradition, Nakwayamtiwa was kikmongwi at Orayvi from about 1850 to 1865 (Titiev 1944:72). A Bear clansman and an albino who never married, he was known as a good chief and a good rainmaker. He was also, in all likelihood, anti-American: in 1858, Lieutenant Ives was received by him in a surly and unfriendly manner (Donaldson 1893:29). Hopi tradition is in accord with the climatic record. The first half of the nineteenth century had been exceptionally wet, comparable in fact to the wet period prior to the droughts which led to the abandonments of Anasazi sites around 1300. The man trained to succeed Nakwayamtiwa died sometime before Nakwayamtiwa's own death, around 1865. Next in line were two brothers, Sakwhongiwma and Loololma. Both were too young to assume the position, however, so their father, Kuyngwu, served as regent kikmongwi and temporary head of Soyal from about 1865 to 1880.

No sooner had Kuyngwu assumed leadership, than the Hopis were devastated by drought and famine. The worst years were between 1866 and 1868, although there had been crop failures as early as 1863 (Whiteley 1988:38). There was also a smallpox epidemic in 1866; whether or not Orayvi suffered as much as Second Mesa, however, is not known. The cause of these disasters, I believe, was not difficult for the Hopis to ascertain. Surely the kikmongwi was to blame. He was not a Bear but a Water Coyote clansman, and it must have been logical to suppose he was an unworthy leader of Soyal. In searching for causes the Hopi could choose between blaming the people or the chiefs. Although most myths mention the people as the cause, there were enough accounts of bad leaders to make this a sensible conclusion in this instance, as the disasters had occurred almost simultaneously with Kuyngwu's assumption of leadership. It is to the kikmongwi's prayers the people attribute the success or failure of their crops, he is responsible for the health and welfare of his subjects, and "in times of trouble, chiefs are often accused of witchcraft" (Titiev 1944:65).

How long it took the disaffected to evolve into a definable group of opponents willing and able to voice their suspicions openly we don't know. By the time of Cushing's visit, though, three developments of note had taken place: (1) Patupha, a Kookop, was recognized as the leader of the Hostile faction; (2) as the two heirs to Nakwayamtiwa grew to maturity, they alternated with each other as kikmongwi and chief of

Soyal; and (3) the position of those opposed to the Bear clan was phrased in terms of a conflict over how to deal with the Americans.

Let us look first at Patupha, the leader of the Hostile faction, to see why a Kookop clansman would assume this role. Cushing identified a "small elderly man" who was the "chief priest of the tribe and a wizard," and who Loololma told him was "Pi-tchi-fui-a, his [Loololma's] would be successor" (Cushing 1922:260, 267). Patupha was in Momtsit but is not mentioned as one of its chiefs. More importantly, he was the last member of the Poswimkya, one of two Hopi curing societies that had been disbanded relatively recently, perhaps even before 1880, since in 1890, only a few older men were still alive who had been members (Stephen 1969:857). The nature and history of these societies and of Hopi shamanism generally are important for an understanding of Patupha's motivations and demand our attention before proceeding.[1]

Hopi healing differed from general North American practices, as well as from those of the other Pueblos, in several important respects. The typical North American shaman received supernatural power from one or more spirit helpers during a vision experience and effected cures by communicating with these supernaturals while in a trance state. It was the trance which set the true shaman off from the ceremonialist (Underhill 1948:36). With the exception of the Hopis, Pueblos organized shamanistic curers into sodalities and vested some curing functions in the hands of the priests of the rainmaking sodalities. The most serious diseases were thought to be of supernatural origin and, of several causes, witchcraft was the most prominent. The belief that disease was caused by intrusion into the body of a foreign object was ubiquitous. The cure by "sucking" or extracting was the most prevalent shamanistic activity. Second in importance was the belief that disease was caused by soul loss.

By contrast, the Hopis did not utilize the trance state, did not have spirit quests or confirmations in sodality initiations or group rites, and did not believe in illness caused by soul loss (Jorgensen 1980:500, 564, 569). They had no curing sodalities and believed that breach of tabu was a major cause of disease, perhaps even more important than witchcraft (Underhill 1948:37). The exceptions to these generalizations, of course, were the two societies discussed below.

Trance states and public performances of shamanistic powers do not seem consonant with Hopi values, which promote cooperation, conformity, and ordinariness. Exceptional individuals, whether shamans, priests, or innovators, tended to be feared. Like other southwestern tribes the Hopis distinguished between natural and supernatural causes of disease. The former were treated by herbalists, bonesetters, and a type of healer with a gift for curing internal disorders by means of massage. Stomach swelling and pain were thought to be caused by the patient's own anxieties or bad thoughts. One officer in each ceremonial society had the power to cure the condition thought to be associated with the ceremony in question. Illness resulting from trespass on the sacred secrets or paraphernalia of the ceremonial societies was supernaturally caused, a breach of tabu; but, as in the case of snake bites cured by the Snake society, it might also occur naturally. The illness controlled by a society was known as its whip (*wavata*). Neither cures performed by societies nor those performed by individuals even suggest the presence of shamanism. The individual healers utilized herbal remedies, bone setting, massage, and "talking"; the ceremonialists used the medicine of their society, prayer, and ritual.

The Hopis, along with the Shoshonean speakers of the Great Basin, were ambivalent about shamans. Supernatural power (*powa*) was neither good nor evil, except as it was used by the one who controlled it. The use of powa for evil purposes by witches was a persistent notion among the Hopi. Its use for good purposes, however, was completely in the hands of the ceremonialists and was denied to the individual curers. The individual Hopi curer was called a *tuuhikya* and did not control powa for healing purposes. His power was called *tuhisa*, a term which Titiev believed also referred to the power a witch received from his animal familiar (Titiev 1943:549). The morpheme "powa" has a limited distribution among the Uto-Aztecan languages, as it is found only among the Numic languages of the Great Basin. The morpheme "tuu," by contrast, is widely distributed and is found far to the south in Tarahumara and Yaqui/Mayo, as well as among the Takic subfamily of languages spoken by the California Uto-Aztecans. Only the Hopi and southern Paiutes use both morphemes. From this I infer that, as Underhill believed, the tuuhikya is a survival of a pre-Pueblo type of curer commonly found among Uto-Aztecan speakers of northern Mexico, southern California, and the Great Basin. As the ceremonial sodalities of the agriculturalist period developed, the tuuhikya was relegated to a subordinate position, and the domain of the newly developed role of ceremonialist was distinguished by the use of the morpheme "powa."

There were, however, two shamanistic Hopi curing societies, the Poswimkya and the Yayaat, which were very un-Hopi in character. These societies were much like those of the Keresans, which appear to have spread to the Tanoans and to the Zunis, and from Zuni to Hopi. Keresan shamans were referred to as "bears," and the bear was the most important tutelary spirit. All Cochiti medicine societies were referred to as Bear societies (Lange 1968:256, 328). The two curing societies of the Tewas were the Cochiti Bear and the Tewa Bear (Dozier 1970:171), and the bear was the tutelary spirit of all Tewa shamans (Parsons 1929:119).The shamans of the most important Zuni medicine societies had the power to impersonate the bear (Bunzel 1932:528).

The diseases cured by the bear shaman societies were those caused by witchcraft, either by means of an intrusive object or by theft of the victim's heart (soul). In addition to performing the sucking cure, these shamans restored stolen hearts by fighting and killing the witch. While in pursuit of witches, shamans could travel immense distances with the aid of the eagle. The curing methods of these societies involved the use of crystals and trance states, sometimes induced by the ingestion of a psychoactive plant.

The Zuni curing societies were borrowed from the Keresans (Eggan 1950:209), and I think it most likely that the Poswimkya and the Yayaat were introduced to Hopi relatively late, perhaps as recently as the early years of the nineteenth century. The traditions of the Poswimkya at First Mesa associated the society with Badger clan, despite the fact that Badger had no proprietary interest in the society (Stephen 1969:860–61). This would be the logical association, since Badger clan members possessed healing powers and served as medicine aspersers in the ceremonial societies. But because the bear was the tutelary spirit of the societies in the other pueblos, it is possible that the society was introduced by Zunis of the Badger clan who are known to have migrated to Walpi during a famine early in the nineteenth century (Kroeber 1917:101). It should also be noted that the bear was a war symbol at Hopi, which may explain the fact that Poswimkya was adopted at Hopi without Bear as a symbol, despite the fact that bear medicines were used in its rituals and cures.

The Hopi Yayaat was a society of wizards who were adept at fire eating, walking on fire, flying, and instantaneously transporting themselves long distances. The name is the Cochiti word for mother, used to refer to the corn fetishes of the medicine societies (Lange 1968:258). The magical feats are identical to those performed by the shamans of the Zuni Fire society (Bunzel 1932:532) and by Keresan and Tanoan shamans generally. The Yayaat was noted for conducting public ceremonies for the entire community during times of drought or pestilence (Beaglehole and Beaglehole 1935:10; Stephen 1969: xii, xl, xlviii, 1007–8). The society was inactive in 1891, when Stephen wrote about them, although several of its members were still living. One of these, who was also a member of the Poswimkya, healed burns. His treatment included swallowing burning embers (Stephen 1969:460). Yayaat shamans had the power to withstand death by fire and falls from heights (Voth 1905: 41–46). According to Titiev (1944:243), the society was controlled by Greasewood clan. First Mesa Hopis told Stephen that the society was *qa hopi*, that is, their practices went against Hopi values and customs (Stephen 1969:1008).

Poswimkya, also inactive when Stephen wrote of them, was a society of sucking shamans. Stephen identified several members from each mesa who still performed cures, however, and the fetishes were still kept in Walpi (Stephen 1969:857). As with the Keresan societies, Poswimkya derived its healing powers from various animals—but with an important difference. Instead of the bear, badger was the tutelary spirit, although bear prayers and medicines were used. Stephen identified Poswimkya with "Posaiyanki," the patron of the Zuni medicine societies (Stephen 1969:281; Cushing 1883:16–18). Despite the fact that Badger was the tutelary spirit of the Poswimkya, there is no indication that either Badger or Gray Badger clans had a proprietary interest in the society. Many Hopis believe the society died out because the requirements of fasting and continence were too rigorous.

Knowledgeable Hopis of today insist that only members of this society could use datura to induce trances or as a medicine. "In times of public distress, famine, sickness, bad crops, or lack of rain, when it was suspected that wizards [witches] had been at work, the Boswimp;kya society held a public curing ceremony to remove bullets that sorcerers had shot into people" (Beaglehole and Beaglehole 1935:9). Society members would have blamed witches (*powaqa*) for the disasters. But if their ministrations were unsuccessful, they themselves might have been blamed for their failure. That their powers were supposed to have been strong enough to counter famine is suggested by an account given to the Beagleholes of

> a famine in which many Hopi migrated to Zuni. The Hopi were weak from starvation. At the first camp on their journey, the people heard a noise like a powerful bird in flight. Two men, the village and the war chief of Walpi, appeared. They were dressed in warrior's costume and they rode on the rattles that sorcerers used to travel great distances. The Hopi were praying for rain. The two wizards worked magic and drew the ground together so that the starving people reached Zuni in two days. (Beaglehole and Beaglehole 1935:10)

There were two surviving members of the Yayaat in Orayvi late in the nineteenth century: Sive'yma, a Kookop like Patupha, and Sikya-hongniwa, who was a Lizard and a member of the Snake society.[2] Both of these men were Hostiles. The two curing societies were responsible for community well-being, and one may suppose they were called upon in 1866. One may also imagine that these "wizards" accused Kuyngwu of witchcraft and that, when their curing magic failed, Bear clan made counter accusations against them. Poswimkya and Yayaat were already feared in all the Hopi villages; for so much supernatural power to be in the hands of individuals was qa hopi.

These two societies were not very long lived at Hopi. My guess is that they drew their membership from less prestigious clans that were hoping to enhance their status. I think that Patupha, a member of a landless "latecomer" clan, felt that his and his clan's status was being eroded. If the shaman societies died and if his magic did not alleviate the drought, the only claim to respect left was Kookop's clan's co-leadership of Momtsit.

Although it is likely that many Hopis still blamed Kuyngwu for the famine and drought, the fact that these disasters had affected First and

Second Mesa as well as Orayvi meant that the issue was not clear-cut and Kuyngwu alone could not be held responsible for such widespread misfortune. On what grounds, then, could the leadership of all the villages be attacked? My speculation is that Patupha and other Kookop men also used their role as warrior guards of the village and their position as co-leaders in Momtsit to justify their opposition to Bear clan and that they sought to gain Spider clan as an ally by finding an issue of importance to both clans.

The target they fastened on was the generally pro-American attitude that seemed to prevail on the other mesas. That the kikmongwis of Orayvi were anti-American was an obstacle that was easy to overcome; the diplomatic strategy followed by Hopi leaders was that of presenting a cooperative and compliant face to any aggressor who appeared stronger than the Hopis in order to avoid open hostilities. The moment an Orayvi kikmongwi was hospitable to any visitor, whether Mormon or other American, he could be tarred with the same brush applied to the leaders of the other villages. In 1882, Loololma had received Cushing hospitably and had pleaded for government protection from his enemies. Third Mesa people had asked the Mormons to settle at Munqapi to help protect them from Navajo depredations, although it is not known whether either Kuyngwu or Loololma was in favor of this.

The War society (Momtsit) is said to have declined in importance sometime during the 1860s, presumably because the government put an end to Navajo raiding (Eggan 1950:100). If this indeed happened, Kookop clan, as co-leader of Momtsit, would have lost all claim to importance. It is, however, difficult to see Orayvis believing that the War society was no longer needed when one considers the troubles they had with the Americans during the 1860s and the fact that the Navajos continued to expropriate Hopi land after their release from Fort Sumner in 1868. By 1871 we find evidence of Orayvi antipathy to the Americans and anger at the Hopis of First and Second mesas for their friendliness with them, as well as some evidence of internal dissention at Orayvi. Agent Crothers noted a "want of harmony among the chiefs, a portion of the chiefs desiring a [census] count taken, and a portion opposing, not wishing to have anything to do with the Americans" (quoted in Whiteley 1988:40). Regardless of what led to the demise of the War societies on First and Second mesas, I think there is some likelihood that factional dissention had something to do with its decline at Orayvi. It also seems likely that Kookop and Spider clans would have opposed those "chiefs" who were willing to have a census taken.

In this context, the myth Patupha told Cushing is interesting. The importance of Spider Grandmother, the wu'ya of Spider clan, in the myths of creation and emergence was not new to the Hopi. There is another account from First Mesa, told to Stephen (1929:3–6) in 1893 by a Haano kiva chief in charge of the fetishes of the Twin War Gods. In this telling, it is the War chief who prays to Spider Grandmother to help the Hopi in the underworld. Spider Grandmother brings them out of the underworld in a reed, and her grandsons, the Twin War Gods, make the upper world safe for habitation by draining the water from the land. The chief of the War society at Walpi also said the War Twins drained the water (Stephen 1929:50–51).

Patupha, as a member of the War society, also emphasizes the Twin War Gods, but he deemphasizes the role of Spider Grandmother by having the Twins bring the people from the underworld without her (Cushing 1923). The Twins also bring fire to the people in the third underworld and drain the water from the present world. Although Spider Grandmother attempts to create light by spinning a cotton mantle, it does not provide enough; a shield is made which becomes the sun, while the mantle becomes the moon. Death (Maasaw, symbol of Maasaw clan and senior clan of the phratry to which Kookop belongs), said Patupha, "is our greatest father and master." Locust was killed but revived himself, thus becoming the medicine of mortal wounds and war. "He is our father too, for having his medicine, we are the greatest of men. Have we not still this medicine? Even though you Americans bring soldiers and slay us, we can defy you, for the locust medicine heals mortal wounds" (Cushing 1923:168). Patupha concentrates on the role of the warrior guards rather than on that of Spider clan, an ally but not yet the leader of the Hostile faction at this time.

The rest of the telling concentrates on the success of the Hopis in resisting their enemies the Navajos and the Mexicans. It ends with a diatribe against the Americans, who are identified with the Pahaana, the older brother who, after the emergence, went to the East but would return to help his poor younger brother, the Hopi. Later, the Hostiles would deny that the Americans were the true Pahaana. Patupha, however, does not, but says that, upon older brother's return,

> You will find me poor, while you will return with the grandeur of plenty, and in the welfare of good food. You will find me hungry and offer me nourishment; but I will cast your morsels aside from my mouth. You will find me naked and offer me garments of soft fabrics, but I will rend your raiments and trample them under my feet. You will find me sad and perplexed, and offer me speeches of consolation and advice; but I will spurn your words, I will reproach, revile, and despise you. You will smile upon me and act gently; but I will scowl upon you and cast you aside as I would cast filth from my presence. Then you will rise and strike my head from my neck. As it rolls in the dust you will arrest it and sit upon it as upon a stool-rock. Then, nor until then, may you feed my belly or clothe my body. But a sorry day will it be for you when you sit upon my head as upon a stool-rock, and a glad day for me. For on that day you will but divide the trail of your own life with the knife which severs my head from my body, and give to me immortal life, liberty, and surcease from anxiety. (Cushing 1923:169–70)[3]

This statement was not a denial of the prophecy, but a challenge to the Americans to fulfill it. According to the prophecy, the Pahaana will return to purify (*powatoqa*) Hopi life; that is, to pass judgment on the witches who have brought so much trouble. They must have their heads "cut off" before the true Hopi way can be restored. Patupha appears to be saying that if the Americans are the true Pahaana they will not be afraid to carry out this task. When he tells the Americans that they must cut off his (Patupha's) head, I do not think he is speaking figuratively as a representative of all Hopi. Instead, I think he is referring to the friendly reception given to Cushing by Loololma: If you are the true Pahaana and ally yourself with Loololma, then it is I, Patupha, who am a witch and whom you must behead.

The last sentence is puzzling, however. How will his death give Patupha "eternal life" and divide the Americans' life? This, I think, makes sense only if Patupha does not really think the Americans are the true Pahaana or that he is one of the witches. Whether or not the White man was the true Pahaana was an issue as early as 1857, when Jacob Hamblin made his first visit to Orayvi. A very old man told Hamblin "that when he was a young man, his father told him that he would live to see white men come among them, who would bring them great blessings, such as their fathers had enjoyed, and that these men would come from the west [sic]." It seems at this time also "a division arose among the men as to whether we were the men prophesied by their fathers, who would come along with them with the knowledge that their fathers possessed" (Little 1909:66). Nor had relations with the Americans been entirely peaceful. During the campaign against the Navajos in 1863, Kit Carson had taken the kikmongwi of Orayvi and another principal man prisoner in the mistaken belief they were allied with the Navajos. As late as 1866, New Mexicans raided Orayvi for slaves, killing several Hopis, taking some boys and girls captive, and stealing over 500 head of livestock (Whiteley 1988:39). There was little reason for the Orayvis to believe that there was nothing to fear from the Americans, and Patupha certainly saw himself in the role of a warrior protecting the village from its enemies.

In sum, there was (1) a legitimate concern on the part of the War society, responsible for protecting the village, and of the War chief (Qaleetaqa) in Soyal whose job it was to advise and even correct the kikmongwi on matters of security; (2) considerable doubt about Kuyngwu's leadership; and (3) Patupha's personal loss of status as a powerful "wizard" in Poswimkya and, perhaps, his apprehension that the War society was also decreasing in importance.

The status of the War society and of the identity of the War chief (Qaleetaqa) in Soyal is problematic. On the one hand, it is possible that the chief of Momtsit was either a Spider or Kookop clansman who also served as Qaleetaqa in Soyal (Whiteley 1988:66, 72–73). If this was the case, Kuyngwu or Loololma gave the position to Badger and Coyote clan after the factional split was well advanced. On the other hand, it is also possible that the office of Qaleetaqa in Soyal was always held by a Badger or Coyote clansman, Kookop and Spider only serving as chiefs of Momtsit (Titiev 1944:60). If so, Momtsit was not a key society. It had a large membership evenly divided between Hostiles and Friendlies and may have declined because of the factional divisions and because it had no important ceremonial function.

A possible clue is found in the list of Hostile leaders named by Loololma during Cushing's visit. The first name on the list was Kui-ian-ai-ni-wa. Parsons identified him as Qöyangayniwa, a Badger clansman who was a leading Friendly and Qaleetaqa in 1893, and who served as the principal Hopi judge by government appointment after the split (Cushing 1922:267n14). If this identification is correct, the position of Qaleetaqa was probably always filled by a Badger or Coyote clansman and Qöyangayniwa changed sides sometime after Cushing's visit.[4]

By the 1880s, then, the Hostiles were led by Patupha of Kookop, who, without yielding leadership to the more prestigious Spider clan, had sought to further legitimatize his position by appealing to the role of Spider and Kookop as guardians and warriors. The rhetoric involved emphasizing their possession of the Twin War Gods as well as of the power of Maasaw. Over the years, Bear clan defended its legitimacy by laying claim to the Twin War Gods as well and by denigrating the importance of Spider Grandmother. The earliest Bear clan telling of the emergence myth was recorded by Voth sometime between 1901 and 1905. Before this, however, the way the leadership was passed from Kuyngwu to his sons looks very much like an acting out of leadership by the Twins themselves.

The two Bear clan brothers alternated as kikmongwi while their father served as chief of the Soyal. Sometime during the late 1870s, Loololma became recognized as the sole kikmongwi and his older brother, Sakwhongyiwma, took charge of the Soyal in 1880. Sharing the duties of the Bear clan chief was not uncommon. While a kikmongwi "rested from his labors" in Soyal or took the time to train a successor, another could serve as Soyalmongwi in his stead. The rotation of the position of kikmongwi is less common, but is explained in this case as the period during which the two brothers were learning and before a final decision had been made. That the responsibility was divided permanently between the two after Loololma became sole kikmongwi is, I believe, somewhat unusual. Loololma was chosen because, of the two, he was the more aggressive. Perhaps, but consider the characteristics of the War Twins:

> They are a pair, not of identical spirits, but more often of opposites . . . there is often the theme of the elder brother who

makes the first attempt, but fails, and the younger brother then succeeds. . . . The Twins are wards of Spider Grandmother who constantly directs them, and saves them from the difficulties that beset them. (Tyler 1964:209, 213)

In fact, it often seems that the younger brother is more successful because he is more impetuous, aggressive, and sure of his actions, although the older brother is wiser and more cautious. The choice of a younger brother was repeated after Loololma's death, around 1904, when Tawakwaptiwa, the youngest of three nephews, became kikmongwi. Loololma had already trained one of the older brothers to succeed him, but this man was passed over in favor of Tawakwaptiwa because the latter was young and "impetuous" (Titiev 1944:83).

Bear clan's claim to the Twin War Gods derives from the nature of the Soyal ceremony itself. Titiev, describing it, says that "we have ample evidence to support the belief that the Soyal is a community ritual, and that it is performed for the benefit of the entire Pueblo. . . . Every important motive of Hopi religion finds expression in one phase or another of the Soyal. The war ritual is for bravery and good health as well as for fighting enemies" (Titiev 1944:144).

The earliest record of Lomahongiwma (Spider) as the leader of the Hostiles is in 1895. By this time, the Orayvis were being pressed to send their children to the government school and the Mennonite missionary, H. R. Voth, had established himself at Orayvi. The Hostiles claimed that Loololma was pro-American and disputed his right to lead. In order to do this, leadership of the faction had to be assumed by a Spider clansman. Not only was it the highest-ranking clan next to, or alongside of, Bear clan, but being in the same phratry it could claim to be a logical successor to Bear. It could also claim to be as important ceremonially as Bear because it controlled more ceremonial societies: Antelope, Blue Flute, and Momtsit.

In 1891, Patupha and Heevi'yma (Kookop) were arrested for a short period, and opposition to the school and to the plan to allot Hopi lands finally convinced the government of the need to send troops to Orayvi. It was during this confrontation that the Hostiles made their formal declaration of war described by Titiev (1944:77–79). Patupha's earlier declaration that "elder brother" would have to behead him was now a possibility. Maasaw, god of fire and death, was impersonated by Patupha; Spider Grandmother was impersonated by Lomahongiwma; and the Twin War Gods by members of the Snake and Lizard clans. Presumably, the war power controlled by Spider and Kookop clans would have been great enough to defeat the troops. After reenforcements arrived, however, the Americans found the village had been evacuated. Nine Hostile leaders were arrested and sent to Fort Wingate, New Mexico. Among those arrested were Patupha, Heevi'ima, Yukiwma, and Talangayniwa (all Kookop); Lomahongiwma and his brother, Lomayestiwa (Spider); Qötswistiwa (Rabbit); and Puuhu'yma (Sun) (Whiteley 1988:80). The leadership was still primarily Kookop, although the two Spider brothers were included. At this time Heevi'yma is referred to as the Hostiles' leader (Whiteley 1988:82).

Heevi'yma and Lomahongiwma were both named as leaders in 1894 after a meeting to discuss the Hostiles' attempt to settle Munqapi (Whiteley 1988:86–87). At this meeting, the Hostile leaders repeated Patupha's earlier contention that the trouble would never be settled unless the government sent troops and, for the first time, threatened to drive the Friendlies "from this country into Mexico." As described in chapter 5, the government did send troops and arrested nineteen Hostiles, who were sent to Alcatraz. The arresting officer, Lieutenant Williams, identified Lomahongiwma as the leader of the faction and Heevi'yma as his principal advisor (Whiteley 1988:88). But he also considered the Kookop men, Patupha, Heevi'yma, and Yukiwma, to be the most subversive.[5]

At some point during these years, the Hostiles set up a rival Soyal ceremony with Lomahongiwma as its chief. Although the Kookops were consistently the leaders, they had arrived at the point where, if they were to challenge Loololma's legitimacy, they had to have a legitimate leader of their own. Lomahongiwma became the Hostiles' kikmongwi, "rather than a de facto leader who achieved prominence by political maneuver" (Whiteley 1988:88). And it is at this time that Voth recorded some myths told by Lomaventiwa, a Bear clansman from Supawlavi (Second Mesa), and Qöyawayma, a Friendly Badger clansman from Orayvi. The role of Spider Grandmother and the Twin War Gods would obviously be a problem for the Orayvi Friendlies and would need to be dealt with in the way they told the myth. We have already seen that, on First Mesa, these deities were important in bringing the people from the underworld. Although both First Mesa tellers, the War chief at Walpi and the Haano kiva chief, were associated with the War society and could be expected to emphasize its importance, we also find Lomaventiwa relating much the same story.

In Lomaventiwa's telling the people are dissolute and the chiefs plan to escape to another world. They also cause a flood which kills many of the people. After the chiefs plant two pine trees, a reed, and a large sunflower in their attempts to climb into the upperworld, Spider Grandmother and the Twin War Gods help the people climb the reed. The final episode is that of the wandering of the various peoples and the White man going to the east to return at such time as the Hopis need him to help defeat their enemies (Voth 1905:10–15). The first death is also attributed to the Bear chief's maternal nephew, presumably Matsito, who is credited with founding Orayvi after a dispute with his brother, the chief of Songoopavi. This is consistent with tradition and shows Second Mesa attitudes toward Orayvi.[6]

Qöyawayma, an Orayvi Friendly who belonged to the Horn, Powamuy, and Snake societies, utilizes the motif of the good and bad creations in order to denigrate Spider Grandmother. Myths of two creators, one good, the other bad, are found among the Maya as well as the Eastern Pueblos and some of the California tribes. In this telling two female deities, a Hard Goods Woman (Huru'ingwuuti) of the East and West, cause the dry land to appear and create birds, animals, and the first human couple from clay. They also teach the humans language and tell them to find a place in which to live. Huru'ingwuuti of the East also creates the White man. Spider Grandmother was living to the south, and she creates the Spaniards. She also makes other human pairs, each speaking their own language.

> All at once she found that . . . there was one more woman than there were men . . . she said "There is a single man somewhere . . . You try to find him and if he accepts you, you live with him . . . The two finally found each other . . . But it was not very long before they commenced to quarrel. . . . They made up with each other, but peace did not last. They soon quarrelled again, separated for a while, came together again, separated

again, and so on. Had these people not lived in that way, all the other Hopi would now live in peace, but others learned it from them, and that is the reason why there are so many contentions between the men and their wives. These are the kind of people that Spider Woman created. (Voth 1905:3–4)

Huru'ingwuuti of the West then created more people who were peaceful, but the people Spider Grandmother created would come among them and cause dissention. At the end of the story, the Spaniards make an attempt on Huru'ingwuuti's life but are unsuccessful. The story of a creation by these two female deities which omits any mention of the emergence is not new among the Hopi; it represents one of the many traditions deriving from the diverse origins which the Hopis tried to harmonize over the years. A similar creation story from Supawlavi makes no mention of Spider Grandmother and her creations (Voth 1905:5–9).

Generally, the various myth traditions were assimilated without difficulty. According to Courlander, however, Huru'ingwuuti is something of an exception: "Her role in the creation or emergence remains in conflict with that of Spider Grandmother" (Courlander 1971:204). She is part of a tradition that has the Hopi coming from the western sea and not emerging from the sipaapuni. This version, Courlander believes, is heard more in Orayvi than it is in the other villages. The concentration of the tradition on one mesa, however, is as likely to be the consequence of factional politics which made its telling more salient in Orayvi than it is to reflect an early western origin of the Orayvis.

In Loololma's version of the emergence as told to Titiev (1944:73–74) by his nephew Tawakwaptiwa, not only are Spider and Bow clans identified as partners in troublemaking in the underworld, but it is Matsito, the Bear clan chief, who executes a successful emergence without the help of Spider Grandmother or the Twin War Gods. In the story of the first death, usually attributed to a nameless witch, Spider Grandmother is identified as the cause of the death of the chief's daughter. Once in the present world, Matsito claims possession of the Twin War Gods and separates himself from Spider Grandmother.

After journeying for some time, Matcito drew on the ground a line running to the east with two forked branches, one pointing north and the other south. "I am going to walk on the path to the south," announced Matcito. "You, Spider Woman, must go to the north. I have no power to feed my people or to bring rain. I have only the Watchmen Brothers [Little War Twins], the Katcinas, and the Soyal ceremony. I think more people will follow you because you can bring rain and make the crops grow, You know how to protect your people from sickness—I have nothing." (Titiev 1944:74)

Here Titiev notes Loololma's message: The gods are more apt to help a poor man, humility is a great virtue, and unusual ability is the mark of a witch. Spider Grandmother then says that she is going north to Kawestima but that some day she will return and will draw Matsito's people away from him until he is worthless. Spider Grandmother's people do return after they find they cannot grow good crops, and Matsito allows them to settle at Orayvi despite knowing that Spider chief will stir up trouble in the future. "Matsito too knew what his destiny was, but he accepted the offers of the Spider leader and allowed his clan to settle at Orayvi" (Titiev 1944:74). The Pahaana prophecy is also related:

When Spider Woman had finished, it was Bahana's turn to speak. "Now I will leave you and travel east," he said, "but I will turn to watch you, Matcito, and I will keep my ears open. If there is any trouble with the Spider Woman, I'll keep watch and help you. You, chief, turn to the east and watch me. We came from the same home—we are not friends but brothers. If Spider Woman makes trouble [witchcraft] I shall return and cut off her head." (Titiev 1944:74)

Because this was told to Titiev by Tawakwaptiwa in the 1930s, we do not know who first enunciated the prophecy that Spider clan would leave Orayvi and return to Kawestima or when Loololma began to speak of the Americans as the Pahaana who would help him against the Hostiles. I think this would have been after Lomahongiwma became leader, however, or Spider Grandmother would not have been singled out.[7]

Before considering what the Hostiles said between 1890 and the actual split, let us review the changes in Hostile leadership that occurred at that time. In 1904 and 1905, Agent Lemmon regarded

Lomahongiwma as the main Hostile leader and Yukiwma as second in importance (Whiteley 1988:100). Yukiwma, however, accused Lomahongiwma of giving in to the Americans and ultimately took his place as leader of the faction. The basis of his claim was, according to Voth (quoted in Whiteley 1988:100), that "although these others were the chiefs, they did not own the village here, and the land, it was I who really owned it, because I represent the old Masauwu." Maasaw was the deity who permitted the Hopis to live on his land in the present world and was the wu'ya of Maasaw clan (also claimed by Kookop because it was in the same phratry). At a meeting at Orayvi day school, Lomahongiwma agreed to let the children go to school, at which point Yukiwma took over leadership formally. Loololma also died at about this time and was succeeded by Tawakwaptiwa. It appears that once Lomahongiwma was made the rival claimant to the village leadership, he immediately adopted the same type of conciliatory diplomacy practiced by Loololma. The kikmongwi is supposed to be the father of his people and to protect them from harm. Spider clan was no longer just the chief of Momtsit but also the cautious and peaceful civil leadership. But it is doubtful that Lomahongiwma really became a Friendly by adopting this stance.

It was also between 1900 and 1905 that Voth (1905:16–26) recorded a myth told by Yukiwma which presented the Kookop position. It is the only version of the creation and emergence in which the chiefs cause the dissention.

> A very long time ago they were living down below. Everything was good there at that time. . . . Everything was good, everything grew well; it rained all the time, everything was blossoming. That was the way it was, but by and by it became different. The chiefs commenced to do bad. Then it stopped raining and they only had very small crops and the winds began to blow. People became sick. By and by it was like it is here now, and at last the people participated in this. They too began to talk bad and be bad. And those that have not a single heart, the sorcerers, that are bad, began to increase and to become more and more. The people began to live the way we are living now, in constant contentions.

The chiefs then plan their revenge upon the people and the emergence takes place. Pahaana is the Bear chief's older brother who goes east but will return to kill the witches and cut off their heads if the Hopi get into trouble. When he does this, Maasaw, who gave them the land, will be chief again, but Bear will be chief until that time. The Bow clan arrived with the Wuwtsim before Bear clan came with the Soyal. The Whites are not the true older brother for whom the Hopis still wait. The witches will side with the false Whites and will want to do whatever the Whites ask of the Hopis.

In this telling we see a recapitulation of history. The blame is laid on the chiefs who caused the end of the wet period, the onset of drought and epidemic, and ultimately the demoralization of the people. The Bow clan's role as ally is reflected by putting it ahead of Bear. And Spider is not given great prominence: the story of the making of the sun and moon is told without mentioning Spider Grandmother, and the coming of the clans of Bear phratry, which includes Spider, is also included. Pahaana, for the first time, is not equated with the Americans, and the alliance between them and the Friendlies is denounced as witchery.

In 1911, after the split had taken place, Yukiwma gave another version of the emergence to Hugh Scott which was published in *Indians of the Enchanted Desert* (Crane 1925) and again by Goldfrank (1948). In this version Yukiwma omits Spider Grandmother entirely and lays the blame for contentions in the underworld on the people rather than the chiefs. The two Huru'ingwuuti help the people climb into the upper world.

> Older brother's people receive the first language, which is that of the White Men. . . . Older brother of chief and his people directed to go to sunrise and stay there. Will be sent for in time of trouble. Chief tells him not to be baptized into any strange fraternity. . . . Older brother travels fast to the east and has not yet returned. . . . Two groups within Ghost [Maasaw] clan: Ghost clan proper and Ghost-and-Bird [Kookop] clan.[8] Known as bravery clan and act as guards. Bear clan and Ghost clan try to win war with Ute, Navajo, and Apache without aid of Ghost-and-Bird clan. Cannot, and ask their aid. Put explosive in pottery;

throw bombs at enemy and scatter them. Then Ghost-and-Bird clan live at Oraibi and are taken into sacred fraternities. Are known as warriors. . . . Traditions say that a stronger people will come upon the Hopi and the Bear Clan will yield. Many years ago Spaniards come from the south and seek to make Hopi accept their ways. Remain four years and the Bear clan yields. Spider clan yields but not Ghost-and-Bird clan. (Goldfrank 1948:248)

The story continues with accounts of how Spider and Bear clans yield to the Spaniards' requests for Hopis to be baptized, and how the Spaniards, aided by First and Second Mesa Hopis and Navajos, battle the Orayvis. Orayvi recognizes that Kookop is the bravest clan, and the people live in peace for many years. When the White men come some Orayvis yield, but not Kookop. It is because of these troubles that Kookop clan leaves Orayvi and settles at Hotvela.

In the end all enemies will combine against Ghost-and-Bird clan. So say the traditions. Youkeoma [Yukiwma] cannot change it nor can he go contrary to the traditions. The talk of white men is incited by witches, and Youkeoma knows that these white men are not the true Bohanna who will come some day and will know the Hopi language. . . . The way for the white men to conquer the Hopis is to cut off Youkeoma's head. The traditions say that the head of one of the Oraibi chiefs will be cut off, and then the troubles will cease. But Youkeoma cannot yield, for then the sea would swallow up the land and all would perish. (Goldfrank 1948:248–49)

The changes from earlier Hostile versions are clear: (1) Spider clan is now no better than Bear clan; (2) the issue, from the very beginning, has always been resistance to enemies, and Kookop has always fulfilled its role as defender of Orayvi; and (3) the Americans are not the true Pahaana, but they will defeat Kookop. We recall that Patupha, too, said that his head must be cut off, but that the Americans' victory would also be his. In sum, even in defeat Kookop has fulfilled its purpose by opposing all enemies of the Hopi, for if it did not do so the people would be destroyed.[9]

The prophecy of the coming of Older Brother is not disputed; instead, the Kookops argue that the Americans are not the true Pahaana. In the twentieth century, the Pahaana prophecy has become very much like waiting for the Messiah. During the Second World War, Yukiwma's son, Dan Qötshongva, thought Hitler might be the Pahaana. German helmets resembled the shape of turtle-shell rattles, and the swastika of the Nazis was like the swastika on Hopi gourd rattles. During the Cold War he suggested that because Russia was in the east, their flag red like the color of the sun, and their helmets like turtle-shell rattles, they might be the Pahaana (Nagata 1978:84–86; Talayesva 1942:379).

The Pahaana prophecy is very much like those of the Toltecs and Aztecs which foretold the return from the east of the cast-out god Quetzalcoatl, and it is found in one form or another throughout the Pueblo world as the "Montezuma myth" (Vaillant 1962:238–64; Parsons 1939:1078-79). It may very well have been current at the time of the Spanish entradas, provoking controversy over the identification of the Spaniards with the Pahaana. The Pahaana prophecy was known and accepted in all Hopi villages and was of sufficient antiquity that it was incorporated into the myth of the emergence. The other prophecies—of a return to Kawestima and the destruction of the ceremonies—pertain only to Orayvi and are more difficult to analyze.

We have seen that the split is thought by some contemporary Hopis to have been a "deliberate plan and that one of its most significant aims was to bring the ritual order to an end, in part because of decadence and corruption" (Whiteley 1988:269). The mythic source of this event is found in the underworld when the disintegration of the social life caused the chiefs to seek an escape to another existence where the Hopi life plan could be reconstituted. In many versions, the most evil people and all but one of the witches are destroyed in the underworld. Thus, the events of the emergence provide the template for a later division of the people as occurred in the splitting of Orayvi. Exactly when such a prophecy was actually formulated is problematic because, if the chiefs plotted the escape, their plan had to be kept secret until the last moment. I can find no reference in the emergence myths that have been published, however, that indicates that the ceremonial system was destroyed. According to Whiteley,

The world had ripened to where events signaled fulfillment of the prophecy on the destruction of the central axis of Oraibi society, its *wiiwimi* or ritual matrix. This prophecy held that after Oraibi's division the ejected party would return to destroy the village completely. The attack was supposed to be launched from the ruined village of Huk'ovi, about two miles to the northwest of Oraibi, which is where the departing hostiles should have gone first. After destroying Oraibi, they would return to Kawestima, making three stops on the way. . . . At Kawestima they would reconstitute *wiiwimi* (particularly the first order societies) on the lines of Oraibi. . . . Meanwhile, if Oraibi was not completely destroyed, it would gradually decay anyway into a ghost town. Sometime in the future, after renewed nomadic migrations with no permanent homes (similar to the period after the Hopi emerged from the world below), people will return to Oraibi, crawling on their hands and knees. After this, Oraibi will rise again to be a flourishing community. (Whiteley 1988:269)

The question is, of course, how much of this prophecy antedates the events of the split and whether it has been changed over the years. In 1894, Heevi'yma threatened to drive the Friendlies out of the village; if there was a prophecy foretelling this we do not know of it. The first mention of a return to Kawestima I have been able to find, although told by Tawakwaptiwa some years after the event, referred to the days immediately before the split in September 1906. The Hostiles had brought allies to Orayvi from Second Mesa in 1904, and had attempted to assign land to them over Tawakwaptiwa's objections. On September 6, 1906, when Tawakwaptiwa tried to expel them, a government official (probably Leupp, according to Titiev) suggested that Yukiwma be approached peacefully and asked to leave Orayvi without making a disturbance. This was "the first time that the chief's narrative indicated a desire to expel Yokioma and the Oraibi Hostiles as well as the Chimopavi [Songoopavi] settlers" (Titiev 1944:85n145).

The next day, the Friendlies decided to try to drive the Second Mesa contingent out: "And if the Hostiles interfered they would turn on them and force them to leave for the north, for Kawestima, where the ancestors of the Spider clan had left the Spider Woman when they went to seek out the Bear clan's settlement at Oraibi"; when the Hostiles tried to help their friends, someone shouted, "They're helping the Chimopovi, now we can drive them all to Kawestima" (Titiev 1944:86).

> Yokioma shouted to his followers. . . . With his big toe trailing in the sand, the Hostile leader drew a line running east and west. To the north of it, facing south towards Oraibi, he grouped his own men, while the Friendlies clustered together south of the line with their backs to the village. Then Yokioma announced the manner in which Oraibi's fate was finally to be settled. "If your men," he said to Tawaqwaptiwa, "are strong enough to push us away from the village and to pass over the line, it will be done. But if we pass over the line, it will not be done, and we will have to live here." (Titiev 1944:86)

If the Hostiles were pushed over the line, which was supposed to represent the Colorado River, they would go north to Kawestima near the Colorado River. "The manner of action decided on by Yokioma was a form of divination to determine whether the moment had come when the Spider Woman's descendents were to draw the Bear chief's followers away from Oraibi" (Titiev 1944:86n149). In the event, the Hostiles were pushed over and left Orayvi to camp a few miles away at the site that became the village of Hotvela. The Friendlies celebrated their victory by holding a Butterfly dance which "had the significance of an earlier scalp dance that used to be performed after a successful raid" (Titiev 1944:87).

Two days after the Hostiles had left, Tawakwaptiwa and other Friendlies told Lemmon "that it was a prophecy that all this would come about and that whichever party was vanquished must leave the village and the Hopi country for ever. That they must go far to the north to the land of Ka-weis-ti-ma, told of in their religious songs" (Whiteley 1988:265). Then, in meetings at Hotvela from October 22 to 25 with Reuben Perry, the Navajo Agency superintendent, Yukiwma said that "all they desire the government to do for them is to return them to the village, behead the Friendly chief, bother them no more about school and let them have their own way. He urged me yesterday and today to cut the Friendly chief's head off and end the trouble" (Whiteley 1988:111).

Whiteley's older informants recall "that the six weeks in camp at Hotevilla before the troops arrived was a period of turbulent discussion. Evidently, Yukiwma wavered: Should they try to return to Oraibi, go on toward Kawestima . . . or begin building at Hotevilla? Finally it was Naquave'ima who made a strong stand to remain at Hotevilla" (Whiteley 1988:112). In the 1980s, the episode was described to Whiteley by a resident of Orayvi:

> It was decided that the only way for the people to survive was to split up. All the chiefs agreed and it was decided on in good faith and with no ill feelings toward each other. Yukioma agreed to lead one group out of Oraibi, and in this way he would fulfill his clan's prophecy of return to their ruins at Kawestima. . . . But Yukioma had a change of heart: he refused to go on his own and carry out his promise. (Whiteley 1988:257)

Whiteley sums up a current Hopi view as follows:

> None of the more sacred ritual practices was to be reconstituted until the Hostiles reached Kawestima (indeed if then . . .) . . . That the possibility of moving on to Kawestima was perceived as real for several years after the split is attested to in missionary correspondence. . . . There was much debate over resumption of Wuwtsim—Yukioma himself was not in favor but bowed to popular demand. (Whiteley 1988:279)

An account recorded in 1974 indicates that there was already, in 1906, the notion that the ceremonies would be discontinued, at least by the Hostiles if not by the Friendlies as well.

> According to Benjamin Wytewa, Sr., whose father was a Spider Clansman, and one of the lieutenants of Yukioma, the chieftain told Wytewa's father in his presence (Wytewa's) that the ceremonial cycle and the ritual cycle had ended with the split at Oraibi, and that he did not want it revived in the new village (Hotevilla). However, at the insistence of former members of the various priesthood societies at Oraibi, he relented and gave his consent. But he predicted that it would not last, since it was

not meant to be, Wytewa said. (*Qua' Töqti*, 12 September 1974, quoted in Whiteley 1988:279)

During the 1930s, Tawakwaptiwa told Titiev that after he had returned from jail and before Lomahongiwma's group left Orayvi for Paaqavi, he had a talk with Kuwannömtiwa[10] when "it was decided that the Chief (Tawakwaptiwa) would continue Hopi ceremonialism while Kuwannömtiwa was to lead his faction to Christianity. But he didn't keep his word and tried to revive Hopi ceremonialism on the pattern of Orayvi."[11] Tawakwaptiwa told Fred Eggan (personal communication, 1988) that the ceremonies had lapsed at Orayvi but would be resumed when the population of the village grew sufficiently to support them. There was no mention of a prophecy that the ceremonial system was to be terminated. Yet today there are many who say that Tawakwaptiwa believed the leadership of Orayvi as well as the ceremonials would die with him. For example, the Hopi newspaper *Qua' Töqti* (10 June 1976) attributes the following statement to Grace Myron, the former wife of Myron Polikwaptiwa. "While Chief Tawaquaptewa had stated earlier that he was grooming Myron Poliquaptewa [Polikwaptiwa] as his successor, shortly before he died the Chief requested that he be buried in the costume of his clan deity, Eototo, which he said would proclaim the end of religion in Oraibi" (Yava 1978:150n59).

Titiev's account differs somewhat, however. Titiev found that "even the great Soyal in which participation was once a badge of manhood and the goal of every male's ceremonial life has been abandoned. At Old Oraibi its leadership used to go hand in hand with the Village chieftainship, but when Tawaquaptiwa began to relinquish that office, he turned more and more duties over to Martin [Myron Polikwaptiwa, Parrot].[12] By 1950, Martin had become the leader of the Soyal, and Tawaqwaptiwa was serving as one of his assistants" (Titiev 1972:338). In 1972, Titiev wrote that

> The political situation at Oraibi is still incompletely settled. Tawaqwaptiwa, the late Village chief, who died on April 30, 1960, was buried by Margaret and Jack. He had belonged to the proper clan (Bear) for chiefs; but since he and his wife, Nasingönsi (Parrot) were childless and since there were no other Bear people at

Oraibi, it was understood that the succession would pass to the Parrot clan through his wife's sister Masamösi. This impression was strengthened when Tawaqwaptiwa adopted three of Masamösi's children, Martin [Myron Polikwaptiwa], Sam [Stanley Paanimptiwa], and Margaret [Mina Lansa], all of whom belonged, of course, to the Parrot clan.

In 1932, Tawaqwaptiwa began to groom Sam and Martin for various Pueblo offices. Inasmuch as Sam was only a boy, most of the functions associated with the Village chieftainship were performed by Martin, and around 1948 the chief let it be known that he was retiring in favor of Martin. Thereupon most of the residents . . . objected violently. They claimed he lacked the proper temperament to be a good leader. . . . Many of those who refused to acknowledge Martin's leadership insisted that their true chief was Sam, even though he was living in Hollywood, California, and in recent years had had only slight contacts with the Pueblo.

While the problem of Oraibi's leadership was so badly tangled, Tawaqwaptiwa, around 1956, suddenly announced that he was resuming the Village chieftainship. Since he was then losing his memory, no one could tell whether he was acting out of mere forgetfulness or out of a recognition of Martin's unpopularity.

By the time Tawaqwaptiwa had died, Margaret, his adopted daughter, had also laid claim to the Village chieftainship. It was understood that her husband, Jack [John Lansa] of the Gray Badger clan, would carry out the masculine duties of the office. There was opposition to this arrangement because it involved a chief of the wrong sex and a male of the wrong clan. (Titiev 1972:344)[13]

Ultimately, Sam and Myron retired from the political arena and the "remaining people of Oraibi rather reluctantly accepted Margaret's leadership. Thus, for the first time in the Pueblo's long history, did most of its inhabitants come to be headed by a feminine chief" (Titiev 1972:345).[14]

There is no direct evidence that Tawakwaptiwa ever thought the ceremonial system was supposed to die out or that he was to be the last kikmongwi of Orayvi. Nor is there direct evidence to support the idea that a prophecy foretold Spider clan's leaving Orayvi for Kawestima. Who was to be ejected from the village was in doubt until the pushing contest decided that it was the Hostiles who were to leave. If the issue was open, why should Kawestima have been an integral part of the prophecy? It was, after all, only in the origin myths of Spider and, some say, Kookop clans and did not refer to Bear clan. Had the Friendlies used it to taunt the Hostiles, saying, in effect, If you don't like it here, why don't you go back to Kawestima?

Once the Hostiles had been driven out of the village it was clear that they were supposed to return to Kawestima, although even then Yukiwma seems not to have been committed to such action. Lomahon-giwma and his followers returned to Orayvi, wishing to forget the whole business, but they were ejected once more and finally settled and founded Paaqavi.

The return to Kawestima never came about. The destruction of the ceremonial system was also not to be, despite the fact that some cere-monies did die out or were not reconstituted in one village or another. Depopulation of Orayvi and acculturative change can account for the post-split history of ceremonies in the various Third Mesa villages as easily as fulfillment of prophecy does. It should also be noted that cere-monies also have been dying in villages other than those of Third Mesa (Levy and Kunitz 1987:936).

The reason for the destruction of the ceremonial cycle is not fully explained by any of the published Hopi accounts. Perhaps it relates to destruction in the underworlds and the need to create the Hopi way of life anew in the present world. If that is so, it is reasonable to see the need to destroy the ceremonial system on Third Mesa and to reconsti-tute it after a new life has been made. The conspiracy theory, of course, rests on an unassailable logic: In order to fulfill the prophecy, the leader-ship had to keep their cabal and the full explication of the prophecy itself secret until after they had accomplished their ends. This is why we hear of these things so long after the fact. It should also be noted that this is the official version, that of the "knowledge-holders," as Whiteley (1988:265) calls them.

Different interpretations may also be dismissed using this explana-tion. A number of commoners (sukavungsinom) were very antagonistic to the leaders of both factions, believing they had not behaved in a responsible manner. Their anger, it is said, was shown *after* they learned the split had been plotted by the chiefs (Whiteley 1988:280). Yet some of the accounts given to me over the years do not mention a conspiracy at all, and one, at least, attributes economic motives to the commoners. According to one Hopi informant, many of the common people resented the pavansinom. Commoners had to work pavansinom fields before they could work their own inferior fields, and when times were hard they were left to fend for themselves. With the split, the common people could find their own fields and farm them without being constrained by clan allotments and control by the pavansinom. "It was then that we could show who the real Hopi were," I was told. The pavansinom were decadent and didn't know how to work; they brought all the trouble on themselves.

That there was a lack of faith in the traditional leadership is evidenced by the conversions to Christianity that took place during the decade following the split. Titiev's census lists 24 Christians. Of these, only one had converted prior to 1906 and only two were Hostiles. Seventeen had been minors in 1900, four were between 18 and 30 years of age, and only three were over 40. Most of the Friendlies went to New Orayvi after the split; five went to Munqapi; and two went to Walpi.

Contributing to the belief that Orayvi ceremonials were destined to be destroyed were the conversions among the Bow clan Friendlies. Kuwanwikvaya (Lizard) had become a Christian prior to 1906. He was married to Nakwahongka (Bow) and was either the father or stepfather of her sons, Johnson Tawaletstiwa and Sikyawaytiwa, who converted to Christianity in 1914. We do not know what led to Kuwanwikvaya's conversion, but it may well have been a reaction to the tribulations of his wife's clan during the years leading up to the split. After the deaths of his maternal cousins, Nasiwaytiwa and Tangakhongniwa, Tawaletstiwa took charge of the Al society paraphernalia. Qötsventiwa, it will be recalled, had been Al chief before but was a Hostile. He revived the society in Hotvela and made replicas of the paraphernalia there. It is commonly believed that Tawaletstiwa had promised to give the original Al materials to Qötventiwa when he asked for them. Instead, after his conversion, he burned them. This act of repudiation of Hopi religion by a member of a high-ranking and priestly clan was later said to have been in accordance with the prophecy that Hopi religion would come to an end at Orayvi.

Finally, let us look at Patupha and Yukiwma, the leaders most often mentioned by outside observers as the most vociferous and troublesome. To the motivations I have already ascribed to them must be added the constancy of their position and their adherence to the prophecies as they understood them. That they were probably reacting to events that diminished their status I have already proposed. At first glance, this may seem to be a demeaning motive rather than an ennobling one. If, however, we consider their message over the years, another picture, not necessarily opposed to the first, emerges.

First, we must recognize that none of the prophecies or myth tellings of the years 1880 to 1910 or so contain anything created de novo. Different elements of the creation and emergence myths may be manipulated to suit the teller's purposes, but none are invented by an individual to fit the contemporary moment. Second, although the origins of each prophecy may be shrouded in the mists of the past, none of the active participants, Friendly or Hostile, deny their validity. Neither Patupha nor Yukiwma deny the Pahaana prophecy. That Yukiwma contends the Americans are not the true Pahaana is, in itself, not new; a similar discussion took place when the Mormons were received in Orayvi in 1857. Even Patupha's position that the Americans, whether the true Pahaana or not, will have to kill him before they can minister to the Hopi is consistent with the Pahaana prophecy. It is repeated later by Yukiwma, but by this time, of course, he has questioned the identity of the Americans and has pointed to the fact that they have tried to missionize the Hopis. At the heart of the matter, in my opinion, is the perception by these men that accommodating the Americans—whether Pahaana or not—involves abandoning the Hopi way of life. Such an event, even in the process of fulfilling a prophecy, would spell the doom of the Hopi. A flood would destroy the present world as it destroyed Palatkwapi and the underworld before that. It is Kookop's destiny to protect the Hopi regardless of events and regardless of the fact that Kookop may be destroyed in the process.

Beyond the fact that the Kookop were the warrior guards of the village, I think it must be conceded that Patupha and Yukiwma were exceptional personalities. Despite arrests and incarceration they remained true to their "mission." Both men were aggressive, perhaps more even than is required of a warrior. Patupha must have been the type of person who was unafraid of his own aggressiveness despite the fact that it was qa hopi. To be a Poswimkya, even after the society became moribund, required him to believe in his powers and to be unafraid of the accusations of witchcraft that would be leveled at him. There are people who use the community's fear of their supernatural power to assert their own deviant personalities, and Patupha, I think, was one of these.

Just how important these individuals were in shaping events may only be guessed at. In my opinion, village fissioning would have relieved population pressure regardless. Munqapi would have been permanently settled by 1900, and Paaqavi, and possibly Hotvela, would certainly have become fairly permanent colonies after the final erosion of Orayvi Wash in 1910. But I think it more likely that the fissioning would have followed the pattern of the colonizing of Munqapi: that is, the creation of daughter villages as on First and Second mesas. Factional dissention there would have been, and probably defections to Christianity as well, but the compromises and diplomatic maneuvers undertaken by both the Bear and Spider chiefs would have maintained a semblance of cohesion. It was Patupha's and Yukiwma's unbending radicalism that made the split so dramatic and final, giving voice to such dire prophecies and, at last, causing the social trauma that has continued to reverberate and shape the political life of Third Mesa.

CHAPTER 8

Conclusions

THE MAJOR AIM OF THIS BOOK has been to examine the Hopi system
of social stratification, first by viewing it as a source of internal contradiction in Hopi social organization, and then by evaluating its role in
the disintegration of the village of Orayvi during the early years of the
twentieth century. To the extent that these tasks have been successfully
achieved, it becomes possible to (1) reexamine Hopi social organization
with a view to clarifying some aspects that have caused confusion in the
past; (2) provide a more comprehensive understanding of the Orayvi
split and its causes, including an integration of Hopi and anthropologists' explanations; and (3) answer some questions arising from generalizations scholars have formulated about the nature of Hopi society
and culture, namely that Hopi social organization was unstable and not
fully integrated.

STRATIFICATION AS A SOURCE OF INTERNAL STRESS

The division of Hopi society into two ranks, or classes, was shown to
derive from an inequitable distribution of the key agricultural resource:
land. Those clans that controlled good land also controlled the most
important ceremonies, and their members were called pavansinom.
Landless clans made up the common people, the sukavungsinom. At

the same time, however, if the society was to survive, a degree of social integration had to be maintained. This was achieved by a number of marriage restrictions that made it virtually impossible for the pavansinom to intermarry, and by opening membership in the clan-controlled ceremonial sodalities to all individuals regardless of clan. Sacred sanction for the social reality was provided by myths and the high value placed on such personal traits as cooperativeness, humility, and pacifism. In effect, the individual was asked to place the demands of the community before his or her own desires.

The quality of the land controlled by a clan was shown to be positively associated with the number of ceremonies and offices it controlled, making it possible to define the social strata in ceremonial rather than economic terms. But the favored economic position of the high-ranking clans was not translated into obvious economic benefits, at least during the period from which our data are derived. The women of the prime and alternate lineages of these clans bore more children than other women, but more of their children died. In consequence, the high-ranking clans were not reproducing themselves and most were in some danger of dying out. Those high-ranking individuals who survived childhood, however, seemed to live longer than those who were less well placed. Thus, although the pavansinom controlled the better resources, they cannot be described as an elite in the sense we usually use the term. There was no economic surplus to speak of, and the pavansinom did not manage or redistribute what surplus there was. The system of social stratification worked to manage scarcity, not abundance. If we cannot characterize the Hopi as egalitarian, by the same token we cannot call them a class society in the sense conveyed by Marx and Lenin.

During periods of scarcity, this system of resource control by a minority made it possible to slough off excess population in an orderly manner. Beyond this, however, it created a tendency to preserve the "core" of every social unit: phratries, clans, and lineages. There was, in effect, no kinship group that was completely homogeneous. Clans within a phratry competed for status and stood ready to take over the position of leading clan in the event the senior clan died out; lineages within a clan were ranked according to their distance from the prime lineage; even households could be strained by conflicting demands made by the lineages of each spouse. Eggan recognized these tensions and noted that they often led to factionalism. Even in the absence of factional division, however, I believe this "fluidity" has caused some confusion when a description of the system is attempted.

Pavansinom and Sukavungsinom

Despite the fact that Titiev, Eggan, and Brandt noted the inequitable distribution of productive land among the clans at Orayvi, they avoided a close examination of Hopi social stratification. Although in theory the idea of two classes is clear, there is, today, a lack of consensus among Hopis about where the lines between the strata are to be drawn. Whether this was also the case in the past cannot be determined with any certainty, but I suspect there was some lack of clarity then as well. Instead of attempting to define strata in terms of the importance of the ceremony a clan controlled, I have relied on correlating the quality of land with the ceremonial position of a clan. By so doing, I have treated the system as a tripartite division of the society when dealing with individuals, but as more of a continuous variable when attempting to rank clans. To the degree that this method replicates the reality, it shows that a simple two-part system was probably never in existence. That social stratification was important in Hopi life, however, I believe has been well demonstrated.

Let us look at some of the problems that make it difficult to draw a definite line between the two classes. Most Hopis with whom I have spoken have insisted that all members of a clan that controlled a ceremony were considered pavansinom. But if this were the case, most of the population would be so considered—even though clans that owned minor, or even what Whiteley has called "second-order," ceremonies did not own viable farmlands. There was also a general feeling that some ceremonies were more important than others. Again, however, there was no consensus concerning this ranking except that Soyal was always given preeminence. Nor is it clear that a clan that owned a ceremony, like Blue Flute, for example, was not considered in the ruling stratum by virtue of the fact that its ceremony was not as important as one of the tribal initiation societies or the Soyal. Although, in theory, all members of a ceremony-controlling clan were pavansinom, large clans had a number of lineages that could never succeed to leadership. This leads one to wonder whether all members of these clans would have been considered pavansinom. There is also the question of the status accorded to individuals of the Gray Badger clan, who might hold the office of dispenser of medicine in a society when there were no Badger clansmen available.

I think it most probable that all members of high-ranked clans were thought of as pavansinom because these clans tended to be small and because they controlled high-quality land. Certainly members of the prime and alternate lineages of middle-ranked clans would be considered pavansinom, but whether or not the marginal lineages would have been included is not clear. These were the larger clans, and their land-holdings were not of the best. It is also doubtful that even the prime lineages of the low-ranking clans were ever thought of as pavansinom, because they controlled no ceremonial positions and had no land.

A number of societies other than Hopi have been noted for a similar lack of precision and clarity; for some of them, this ambiguity has been seen to have a certain functional utility. Vidich and Bensman (1958) have noted the differing emic definitions of stratification hierarchies in the United States, and the ambiguous nature of the caste system in Ceylon has been explicated by Tambiah (1965). Differing views of the stratification system permit individuals and even groups to define their status to suit themselves, despite the fact that the community as a whole may not agree. The illusion of status makes it easier for individuals to feel they are a part of the system. Perhaps even more important, however, this ambiguity permits groups to negotiate for improved status and thus legitimatizes some upward mobility. As James West (1945) found in Plainville, only those at the very top and bottom would tend to see the hierarchy in the same way. Those in the middle could identify with those at the top or even use different criteria for ranking. As some clans grew and others died out, the lack of a rigidly defined system allowed clans more freedom in their jockeying for position. Kookop clan, for example, was able to claim the wu'ya of Maasaw, the senior clan of its phratry, to enhance its position without exciting great opposition to its claims.[1]

Households, Lineages, Clans, and Phratries

There has been some confusion in the anthropological literature concerning Hopi phratries, clans, lineages, and households. Lowie (1929: 330) defined a matrilineal lineage as a group of matrilineally related kin descended from a common, known ancestress, and found between one and five distinct lineages in each named clan. Parsons (1925:15, 1939: 60), however, confused phratries with clans and labeled clans as lineages or maternal families. Titiev clarified the distinction between clans and phratries in a satisfactory manner but introduced a new element of confusion when he talked about a "household group" as a segment of a lineage.

Calling these lineage segments "households" or "household groups" creates the possibility of confusion because a descent group is conflated with a residential group. In chapter 3 we saw that, when viewed across several generations, a lineage conformed to Lowie's definition but that, in each generation, the position of the women shifted. The daughters of a clan mother were all in the prime lineage as long as their mother lived; after her death, however, one daughter headed the prime lineage while the others headed alternate lineages. In the next generation, the children of the alternate lineages became adults of marginal lineages. The question then is whether these "lineages," as Eggan, Connelly and I call them, or "lineage segments," as Titiev has referred to them, are better thought of as households.

We have seen that only about 24 percent of Hopi households in 1900 comprised matrifocal, extended families and that about 54 percent were nuclear families. Because married daughters eventually established households of their own, and because the daughter chosen to become clan mother returned to her natal household to assume her responsibilities, the ties which bound this lineage together crossed household boundaries. As males continued to have responsibilities to their sisters' children, to perform ceremonial duties, and sometimes to retain use rights to fields controlled by their mother or sisters, it is more accurate to see them as members of their lineage and not as nonresident members of a household. The functioning group was the lineage—not simply a group of coresident kin who may or may not comprise the whole lineage but are almost always a segment of it. It seems to me that

Eggan was correct when he spoke of the lineage principle: The household was the basic economic unit, but the transmission of property and rights was handled by what I have called the lineage and what Titiev thought of as a segment of a lineage.

Not only did prime and alternate lineages behave differently from marginal lineages, but the importance of the lineage varied with the ranking of the clan. I suspect this variability is also a source of confusion, as members of lower-ranking clans may place less emphasis on lineage functions because they were less important in their lives. At the present time, clans no longer control agricultural lands and only the oldest Hopis from Orayvi are likely to emphasize the role of lineages in controlling and transmitting land. With the disappearance of the economic functions of the lineage, the household structure of today has become "bilaterally oriented" (Nagata 1970:223–87). Maternal uncles play a smaller role in rearing and disciplining their sisters' children, and even cooperation in farming tasks is more a matter for the nuclear family than for the lineage. In consequence, it is difficult for the contemporary observer to discriminate accurately among lineage and household functions.

A dynamic balance was maintained between the divisive force of the inequitable distribution of the agricultural resource and the consequent system of stratification on the one hand, and the unifying forces of village endogamy, a variety of exogamic marriage rules, open membership of the ceremonial societies, and the ideological system on the other. Together, these opposing tendencies enabled the village to survive periods of severe economic deprivation as well as contact with outsiders.

Causes of the Orayvi Split

The importance of economic distress as a cause of the Orayvi split was verified by the fact that high-ranking clans and the prime and alternate lineages of middle-ranking clans tended to remain in the Friendly camp, while the landless clans and the marginal lineages of middle-ranking clans joined the Hostiles. The prolonged dry period that lasted with very little respite from 1865 to and beyond the year of the split—in conjunction with the growth of Orayvi's population—appears to have been the major cause of the final dissolution of the village. Although Munqapi provided fields for a number of low-status families that remained loyal to the village chief, Mormon encroachments placed limits on the number of landless people who could settle there. That households moved as units was not, as Titiev thought, due to the influence men had over their wives but to the long period of dissention which provided ample time for politically compatible marriages to become the norm. Even disapproved marriages into father's clan and phratry were made for political purposes.

Before accepting this explanation, however, we must ask why Orayvi was the only Hopi village to fission in response to these pressures. The long period of drought at the end of the century affected the whole area, and Polacca and Wipho washes had been degraded by erosion before Orayvi Wash. The villages of First and Second Mesa had been affected by the smallpox epidemics, and Navajo depredations impinged upon the movements of Hopis from all mesas. There was, moreover, dissention in most if not all of the villages. Pro- and anti-American factions are documented at Second Mesa and hinted at in Walpi. In that village there was politicking and opposition when the Americans wished to make Polacca, a Haano Tewa, chief of the entire mesa, and a Second Mesa priest told Stephen that the rains didn't come to Walpi because there was dissention in the village (Stephen 1969:1022). The crucial difference between Orayvi and the other villages was the land-to-population ratio. Erosion had not proceeded as far at Orayvi as at the other mesas, and Orayvi had not been hit as hard by smallpox. Orayvi, therefore, attracted refugees from the east and also had a higher natural rate of growth. It was the growing population that placed the great strain on the land resource. Declining populations on the other mesas had plenty of farmland; on Third Mesa it was in short supply.

In light of the foregoing, is it possible to think of Hopi social organization as fragile? Can one not as easily argue that it was resilient? Only one village disintegrated, after all, and the split was arguably an adaptive response. The sloughing-off of excess population preserved the core and permitted new, independent settlements to be formed. The hierarchical organization, it would seem, had performed its function admirably. Moreover, it took a full 50 years from the time of the first drought and famine in 1866 to the final dissolution of the village in 1906.

Nor do I think history suggests that the Hopi people were more anxiety ridden or maladjusted than inhabitants of small and poor villages in many parts of the world. Village factions, gossip, witchcraft accusations, and the like are not found only among the Hopis. Of course, the very long period of economic and acculturative stress from the middle of the nineteenth century through the Great Depression and the Second World War may have made anxiety more visible to observers—and thus more likely to be commented on than if the observations had been made before or after this time.

Cycles and Prophecies

We have seen that the Hopis have a cyclical view of history and have explained the Orayvi split as the culmination of a series of events presaged by past cycles, indeed foretold by them.[2] At first glance, Hopi explanations appear quite different from those offered by anthropologists. Those prophecies made before the events in question, such as the return to Kawestima and the destruction of Orayvi, never came about. The veracity of prophecies announced after the events in question, for example, the alleged foretelling of the demise of the ceremonial cycle at Orayvi, depends on one's acceptance of the cyclical nature of history: It must have been foretold because it happened. The belief that the split was plotted in secret by the pavansinom of both factions rests especially on the fact that a number of myths account for similar disasters in this way. Taking only the prophecies into consideration, one is tempted to conclude that they are used to account for events in such a way that the pavansinom are not discredited. To let matters rest at this, however, would obscure some of the real similarities between Hopi and Western modes of explanation, as well as some of the real differences.

Turning our attention first to similarities, there is no need to debate the fact that cyclical notions of history have been powerful in the West from the time of the Greeks to the present, despite the addition of such notions as evolution and progress introduced initially by Saint Augustine. The Greeks developed their ideas about the cycles of history from the metaphor of organic growth: the notion that societies, like plants, contained the seeds of their entire life cycle from birth and that their growth, maturity, and decline were inherent in their very nature.

In fact, according to Nisbet (1969:7), "Of all metaphors in Western thought on mankind and culture, the oldest, most powerful and encompassing is the metaphor of growth." The Hopi agricultural cycle, we have seen, is the basis for the cycle of the ceremonial year, and Hopi historical cycles proceed from establishing the proper social forms to their decay and final destruction. The organic metaphor is not adhered to as closely by the Hopis, but neither does it diverge widely from it. Plato, for example, believed that eternity is an endless succession of cycles which are very similar to those described in Hopi myths.

> Invariably one of these cycles is held to terminate in some great catastrophe, usually a flood . . . with but a handful of individuals left alive to commence the next cycle of civilization. . . . Plato speculates on the possibility of a "few shepherds, high in the hills" surviving the flood that has wiped out the rest of mankind and all its institutions. From these few simple, unlettered, and good individuals, . . . a new cycle of civilization begins. (Nisbet 1969:37)

In more recent times, the cyclical rise and fall of civilizations has been espoused by such historians as Spengler, Toynbee, and Sorokin; and the popular notion that history repeats itself reminds us that our own views are not totally at odds with those of the Hopi. But the metaphor of growth and decay as applied to societies and cultures, as Nisbet (1969:267) has observed, has relevance and utility only insofar as it is applied to "constructed entities: to civilization as a whole, to mankind, to total society." The imposition of these grand concepts on the "social behavior of human beings in specific areas and within finite limits of time" (Nisbet 1969:267), however, is not appropriate because the purpose of the concepts is to ascertain the natural path of change and not the actual sequence of events as affected by random events. Yet the Hopis appear to explain specific changes such as the Orayvi split in just such terms. In doing so, they are not much different from many neo-evolutionists and functionalists. Whiteley (1988:283) has pointed out that the specific events and their causes—"population pressure upon waning resources," and so on—were recognized at the time of the split but were not taken into account when the larger meaning of these events was sought.

Hopi modes of explanation differ from ours in two respects: the direction of the causal arrows, and the penchant for casting all political statements in terms of prophecy. Yukiwma, for example, recognized the contribution of drought and famine to the social unrest and political dissention in the village. But where a Westerner would attribute such events to "natural" causes far removed from the control of humankind, Yukiwma saw them as the direct consequence of the moral actions of the village leadership. In this respect, Hopi views of causality are like those of all preindustrial societies and, as such, are neither novel nor demanding of further discussion.

The use of prophecy appears to be a cultural style consonant with the conservative tenor of Hopi society and the place of the individual within it. In most North American Indian societies it was considered proper for an individual to have a personal "vision," a direct contact with the realm of the supernatural. An emerging leader could announce his vision and ask his supporters to follow him. The rise of such movements as the Handsome Lake and Ghost Dance religions are cases in point. Among the Hopi, however, the individual can have no direct contact with the supernatural, personal visions are discountenanced, and innovation distrusted. All reevaluation of the social and political reality must be expressed in terms of cultural precedence; that is, as fulfillment of prophecies and examples of the unfolding of new cycles or the termination of old ones.

Given these constraints, it is not surprising to find the phrasing of prophecies changing as events unfold and the creation and emergence myths being manipulated to suit the purposes of the teller. Such manipulations should not be seen as the cynical products of politicians. If all members of the society share this view of history then the individual justifies himself to himself as well as to the community; and we note that neither in the telling of prophecy nor of myths are themes or motifs introduced de novo. Events that seem to deviate from the expected unfolding of the cycle are seen as fortuitous, but do not contradict or disprove the theory.

It was Malinowski (1926) who first proposed that origin myths contained the legal charter of the community, giving sacred sanction to the status quo. The events described in this chapter illustrate how myths may, indeed must, be adjusted and fashioned to suit changing social

conditions and, especially in the case of the plot concocted by the pavansinom of both factions, to provide acceptable justifications for dis-
turbing events in a manner that allows the traditional social system to
continue.

Throughout the history of the split, kikmongwis and Hostile
leaders alike behaved in a consistent manner. The kikmongwis, including the Spider contestant, always acted in accordance with the long tradition of Hopi diplomacy which demanded they protect their people
from destruction at the hands of outsiders. The leaders of the Hostiles,
we have seen, were members of a low-ranked clan, Kookop, that was
losing its two claims to status: membership in a recently adopted curing
society and co-leadership of the Warrior society. The Hostiles represented those Hopis most hurt by the decline of agricultural production.
They found a cause for this decline and sought to change things, first
by proposing a new but legitimate leadership, then by attempting to
expel the Friendlies who were identified as the cause of the troubles,
and finally by leaving the village entirely. That the followers of Lomahongiwma of Spider clan sought a reconciliation and a return to Orayvi
further emphasizes the importance of social stratification in the history
of the Orayvi split.

Clan Lands Identified
by Bradfield and Titiev

Clan lands were assigned a score according to their quality, as described in chapter 3. The description and location of the fields is based on the map and information provided by Bradfield (1971:46–51). The location symbols are those used by Bradfield on his map in the end pocket of that volume. Clans are grouped by phratry.

Bear. Located at the head of the floodplain, with no mention of size; but Titiev shows it as being enormous. Of course, plots of this land went to various priests of other clans. This was the very best land of all. **Score = 4**

Spider. Bradfield thinks Spider land was at H3.62 (these are the location symbols used by Bradfield on his map), a fairly large fan of a tributary watercourse just north of Bear land. Titiev says Spider clan got a small portion of Bear clan land for helping in Soyal (as War chief). Bradfield does not show it, and Spiders complained of their allotment during the split years. I am assuming they had some Bear clan land, as well as other land as shown by Bradfield.

Score 2 + 1 = 3

Katsin. Perhaps shared land with Parrot (there were only 11 people in the clan) on the tributary fan at J2.42. **Score = 2**

Parrot. Titiev shows Parrot land (J2.42) near Reed and Badger on the fan of a major tributary. Parrot also had a portion of Bear clan land on the east side of the wash. **Score 2 + 1 = 3**

Rabbit (Tobacco). Rabbit clan land lay within the fence at I3.27. It was on a side valley slope with a minor runoff watercourse and no fan. Rabbit also had a plot of Bear clan land because it supplied the Tobacco chief for the Soyal.

Score 1 + 1 = 2

Snake. Titiev shows Snake owning land next to Bow at the bottom of the floodplain.

Score = 3

Lizard. Titiev places Lizard lands above those of Hawk on the same tributary watercourse (F2-F3). There is no fan, and the fields are quite small. **Score = 1**

Sand. The land was on the east side of the valley, on the tributary watercourse traversing G4. It seems to have received runoff directly from the side valley slope, and there was no fan.

Score = 1

Reed. According to Bradfield, Reed land was below the mesa to the southwest of the village, possibly along the watercourse at J3.29 adjacent to Greasewood. This is side valley slope with some runoff channels but no fan. Although Titiev places Reed lands next to the Badger field at J2.62, which is a fan at the bottom of a tributary watercourse, it is hard to conceive of clans of different phratries sharing, so I opt for the former location. **Score = 1**

Greasewood. This land was below the mesa to the southwest of the village, possibly along the watercourse at J3.29, adjacent to Reed (side valley slope). It also had a plot of Bear clan land because it supplied the Crier chief for the Soyal.

Score 1 + 1 = 2

Bow. Placed by Titiev next to Lizard along watercourse F2-F3.11, and low down on the main floodplain in the vicinity of the lower windmill. **Score = 3**

Maasaw. Neither Bradfield nor Titiev identified any Maasaw lands, but I am fairly sure that since Maasaw had taken over ownership of the Kwan society and Kwan clan was not represented at Oraibi in 1900, Maasaw had also taken over the Kwan lands between Eagle and Hawk (D3.42) on the fan of a tributary watercourse (probably two fans at the ends of two parallel courses). **Score = 2**

Kookop. Shown by Titiev as owning land below the mesa at about I2.68 at the foot of the talus slope below a spring. Used for orchards today. **Score = 1**

Coyote. Bradfield locates the land along the tributary watercourse at J3.64, downstream from Badger fields on a fan and from Greasewood and Reed fields on another watercourse. It is not clear if there was a fan, but as the watercourse emptied onto the floodplain I assume there was one. **Score = 2**

Water Coyote. No lands have been identified, although this was a large clan.

Score = 0

Millet (*leehu*). No lands have been identified. This was a very small clan.

Score = 0

Agave (*kwan*). Bradfield and Titiev locate the fields between Eagle and Hawk on the fan of a tributary watercourse (D3.42). As there were no people in this clan in 1900 and Maasaw had probably taken over the fields, I have assigned no score.

Score = 0

Badger. Located along the tributary watercourse at J2.62, a fairly large fan on a major tributary.

Score = 2

Gray Badger. No lands identified.

Score = 0

Navajo Badger. No lands identified.

Score = 0

Butterfly. No lands identified.

Score = 0

Patki. On the floodplain just below Rabbit. Also had two farms on Bear land, one for participation in Soyal, another for impersonating Aholi.

Score 3 + 1 = 4

Piikyas. Bradfield and Titiev locate some land on the east side of the main wash opposite Eagle, Kwan, and Hawk. These fields were at the foot of the talus slope. Some fields on this side of the wash may have belonged to Second Mesa. Titiev also shows some land west of Kookop land at J2.39, also valley slope.

Score = 1

Rabbitbrush (*sivap*). No lands identified.

Score = 0

Squash. Titiev places this clan with Hawk on a fan of the tributary watercourse that traverses F3, south of the middle windmill.

Score = 2

Hawk (*kyel*). On a fan of the tributary watercourse traversing F3, south of the middle windmill.

Score = 2

Crane. No lands identified.

Score = 0

Sun. No lands identified (but a large clan population).

Score = 0

Eagle (*kwaa*). From D3.58 downstream on the west side of the wash, at the foot of a talus slope.

Score = 1

Bluebird. Bradfield locates Bluebird land on the east side of the floodplain above Parrot. There was no Bluebird clan in Orayvi, so this land may have belonged to Songoopavi.

Free Land. This was a large stretch of ground on the west bank of Orayvi Wash, stretching from the old road to Songoopavi upstream to where the Mennonite school now stands, with its apex at the spring at New Orayvi. This is all side valley slope without springs or tributary watercourses.

Appendix B

Clan Ceremonial Scores

3 points: Ownership of a major ceremony. These ceremonies were always in the charge of a secret society.

2 points: (a) Ownership of a major political office. In addition to the Village chief, these were the five officers of the Soyal who assisted in this ceremony and held the "chiefs' talk"; (b) ownership of a ceremonial kiva.

1 point: (a) Ownership of a "common kiva"; (b) ownership of an extinct or "minor" ceremony; (c) right to impersonate a Mongkatsina; (d) ownership of a minor ceremonial office.

Bear. Major ceremony = Soyal; major political office = Village chief; chief katsinas = Soyal and Eototo. **Score = 7**

Spider. Major ceremonies = Blue Flute, Antelope, Momtsit; major political office = War chief; ceremonial kiva = Blue Flute; common kiva = Wiklovi. **Score = 14**

Katsin. Common kiva = Katsin; minor ceremony = Niman.[1] **Score = 2**

---

[1]Katsin shares control of the katsina cult with the Badger clan, yet it controls no secret society as does Badger. It is in charge of the summer katsina performances and controls Niman, the Going Home dance. I have opted to score this as a minor ceremony, but it might well be thought otherwise. Whiteley believes it to be a ceremony of the third (lowest) rank.

Parrot. Major ceremonies = Tao, Lakon; major political office = Soyal; ceremonial kiva = Tao. **Score = 10**

Rabbit. Major political office = Soyal. **Score = 2**

_____

Snake. Major ceremony = Snake; ceremonial kiva = Snake. **Score = 5**

Lizard. Major ceremony = Maraw; common kiva = Maraw. **Score = 4**

Sand. Major ceremony = Oaqöl. **Score = 3**

_____

Reed. **Score = 0**

Greasewood. Major political office = Soyal Crier chief; minor ceremony = Yayaat (extinct). **Score = 3**

Bow. Major ceremony = Al; ceremonial kiva = Nasavi; minor ceremonial office = Sunwatcher, cistern opener. **Score = 7**

_____

Maasaw. Major ceremony = Kwan; ceremonial kiva = Kwan. **Score = 5**

Kookop. Minor ceremony = Stick swallowers (extinct). **Score = 1**

Coyote. Common kiva = Pongovi and Coyote. **Score = 2**

Water Coyote. **Score = 0**

Millet. **Score = 0**

_____

Badger. Major ceremony = Powamuy; ceremonial kiva = Hotsivi; chief katsina = Ahul and others. **Score = 6**

Gray Badger. **Score = 0**

Navajo Badger. **Score = 0**

Butterfly. **Score = 0**

_____

Patki. Major ceremony = Gray Flute; major political office = Soyal; chief katsina = Aholi; minor ceremonial office = Sunwatcher. **Score = 7**

Piikyas. **Score = 0**

Rabbitbrush. **Score = 0**

_____

Squash. Common kiva = Haano.   **Score = 1**

Hawk. Major ceremony = Wuwtsim.   **Score = 3**

Crane.   **Score = 0**

———————

Sun.   **Score = 0**

Eagle. Minor ceremony = Paiyatemu.   **Score = 1**

Notes

CHAPTER 1

1. The original field notes are located at the Peabody Museum of Archaeology and Ethnology, Harvard University, Cambridge, Massachusetts.

2. This plan was published by Victor Mindeleff (1891) and Cosmos Mindeleff (1900). I have used a copy of Titiev's original plan with his household identification provided me by Catherine M. Cameron.

CHAPTER 2

1. Some have even placed the date as late as A.D. 1000 (Wright 1978).

2. Clan, as used throughout, is more properly Murdock's "sib," a unilineal descent group, the members of which "acknowledge a traditional bond of descent in the maternal or paternal line, but are unable always to trace the actual genealogical connections between individuals" (Murdock 1965:47). Membership in a sib is retained even though residence may change after marriage. A clan, by contrast, is what Murdock calls a compromise kin group based on both a rule of descent and a rule of residence (Murdock 1965:66). In this instance, an in-marrying spouse becomes a member of the clan upon changing residence at time of marriage.

3. Given that it was the women who owned the land, one might expect that most of the farm work would have been done by them, a pattern found among all the matrilineal tribes of the Eastern Woodlands. Among the Pueblos, however, this work was done by men and we can only speculate on how this came about. It is possible that prior to A.D. 1200 women did most of the farming, but

that as the environment deteriorated and competition for resources increased men took over the task. It is also possible that the transition occurred after the Spanish entradas, when the villages along the southern edge of Black Mesa were relocated from the valley floor to the mesa top for reasons of security.

4. Today, children as young as eight or nine years of age are initiated into the katsina society.

5. General descriptions of various aspects of Hopi world view as expressed in the ceremonial cycle and myths have been provided by Titiev (1944), Hieb (1979), Frigout (1979), Courlander (1971, 1982), and Kennard (1972).

6. These accounts may be found in Courlander (1982) and Voth (1905). The sites of Payupki and Sikyatki are known archaeologically. Whether the abandonments were due to dissolution or to the drying up of the springs, as in the case of Payupki, is not known. Palatkwapi, though Hopis locate it south of the Little Colorado River, seems almost a memory of the flooding that caused the abandonments of villages situated along that river.

CHAPTER 3

1. The analysis of Hopi fields is based on that of Bradfield (1971).

2. Bradfield refers to fields made on the fans of watercourses and on the floodplain of Orayvi Wash by the Papago word, *ak'chin*.

3. It is not entirely clear whether some of the Bear clan fields assigned to various clans represent their clan allotment or a particular field assigned to the individual in charge of a specific ceremonial function in the Soyal ceremony. Rabbit and Parrot clans, for example, held land on tributary watercourses as well as fields of Bear clan land. Patki (Water House) clan had a large tract of land on the lower half of the floodplain but also had a much smaller piece of land higher up in the Bear clan fields as well as a plot for the Ahöla impersonator. Although Titiev shows Spider clan as holding only a small tract within Bear clan land, which might suggest that this was their entire allotment, Bradfield places their land somewhat to the north. According to Titiev, Bear clan lands were allotted to the War chief, who aided the village chief in the performance of the Soyal ceremony, and to the other officers and men who participated in that rite (Titiev 1944:62). These special plots were supposed to be held by Soyal officers only during their term of office, and disputes often arose when retiring officers refused to cede their lands to their successors.

Titiev says that Piikyas (Young Corn) clan head was a Soyal officer, yet his clan land map shows Patki controlling the land within the Bear clan holdings. Similarly, Titiev was told that the War chief was either a Coyote or Badger clansman. Yet the War society (Momtsit) was jointly owned by Spider and Kookop clans. In this instance it appears that the Village chief was describing the situation after the development of the factions and the demise of the War society. There is also the question of whether or not Bear clan lands were assigned to the priests of the other important ceremonies, specifically the societies of the tribal initiation. Titiev notes this omission, but does not say whether these chiefs were traditionally allotted fields within Bear clan lands. If they were and the chief saw fit to omit them, it may have been because of the way these societies affiliated themselves during the split.

4. Bradfield's (1971) estimates are slightly different from those provided by Stephen (1969:954–55), who, he felt, assumed that a higher proportion of the harvest was kept for storage than was actually the case.

5. Hegmon used the field strategies and field types described by Forde (1931) for First Mesa in 1928. The floodplain of the Polacca Wash had been cut down for a long time and the fields utilized were those of medium and poor quality on the fans of the tributary watercourses and the side valley slopes of the mesa. Hegmon's model then would fit all the Orayvi fields except those on the floodplain of Orayvi Wash, where the yields would have been more secure and abundant.

6. Despite the fact that the War society (Momtsit) was, at one time, a major society, I have given it the score of a minor ceremony. The War society became moribund around 1860, after actual Navajo raiding came to an end (Eggan 1950:100). According to Titiev (1944:155–63), there were two warrior organizations at Orayvi: The "ordinary" warrior society, or Momtsit, which was divided into two groups, the Momtsit and the Stick Swallowers; and the "real" warriors whose members had to kill and scalp an enemy. Momtsit and Stick Swallowers performed their ceremonies in Wiklavi kiva. Whether the fact that the "real" warriors were initiated in Hawiwvi kiva justifies classing them as a separate society is moot. Spider and Kookop clans shared in the control of Momtsit as well as the "real" warriors. It is most likely, in my opinion, that there was one War society with different orders. Virtually every young male was expected to join Momtsit, although few ever took an enemy's scalp. That Coyote and Badger supplied the War chief in Soyal by around 1900 may have been a consequence of the factional split which set Spider and Kookop against the Village chief. Although Momtsit was still in existence in 1900, there were no longer any "real" warriors, and the society had declined in importance and did not survive the splitting of the village in 1906.

7. Lineage as used here refers to Titiev's lineage segment and household group. The reasons for doing this are discussed in chapter 4. Individuals were located on Kennard's genealogies and their lineage position determined wherever possible. Titiev's data gave many of the clan mothers, but also gave the ceremonial offices held by both men and women. For some clans the position of clan mother over the generations was inferred from the positions held by males of succeeding generations and by those held by the women. Women's

ages and number of children born and surviving come from the enumerators' schedules of the 1900 census.

8. This is a rather crude measure. Women were asked how many children they had borne and how many were still surviving. There is no information concerning age of death, number of still births, or spontaneous abortions.

9. By comparison with the Navajos on the Hopi reservation in 1900, the Hopis generally had higher fertility rates but very much poorer survival rates of children among women 33 years of age and above (Johansson and Preston 1978).

10. The mean ages of women heading the other forms of household were virtually the same as those heading extended households: 40.7 years.

11. Lineage affiliation was also an important determinant of political affiliation during the Orayvi split, as we shall see in the discussion of the split.

12. Bradfield identifies the free land as "the area of the old farm land on the west bank of the main wash, stretching from the old road to Shungopavi [Songoopavi] upstream to where the Mennonite school now stands, with its apex at the spring at Kyakots'movi [Kiqötsmovi] (New Orayvi)" (Bradfield 1971:51). These are the fields listed by Bradfield on the bottom of his page 47: in the column of fields still in cultivation—from the large fields below Kiqötsmovi school to the bottom of the column; in the column of fields gone out of cultivation—from abandoned field, G3.72, to and including the area in the bend of the wash, H3.76, which is the largest plot (42 acres).

13. Eggan (1967) tells the story of the decline of both Bear and Spider clans at First Mesa and how the clans of the Snake and Horn phratries competed to assume leadership of the village.

Chapter 4

1. The proportions for men are virtually identical.

2. Another five had remarried after having been widowed.

3. The study included suicides and deaths from alcoholic cirrhosis between 1955 and 1964. The parents of the generations studied had married sometime between 1880 and 1930 and so include families formed during the period under discussion here and thus represent, in part, the more traditional patterns.

4. Although the Hostile faction had duplicated several ceremonial societies before 1906, these have not been tabulated here. On the other hand, there is no mention in Titiev's census of Spider clan's position in the Soyal. Spider clan, as controller of the War society, would logically have provided the War chief for the Soyal society. Instead, a Coyote man was named. This is either a reflection of bias on the part of the chief or a reflection of some confusion on Titiev's part concerning the recruitment of the War chief. Titiev (1944:60) says that the office of War chief was held by either Coyote or Badger clan, implying that the War

society was not involved in the Soyal even before the development of the factions. Overall, the pattern of membership pertains to the situation prior to the establishment of the parallel ceremonial system by the Hostile faction.

5. Although the total number of society memberships was tabulated for each individual, a maximum of three was listed by name. There were a very few individuals who had membership in four societies, not enough to change the pattern revealed in the figures.

6. As all males were initiated into one of the tribal initiation societies, most often the Wuwtsim, this society was not counted in the number of societies joined. And because everyone was initiated into the Katsina society, only men who were noted in Titiev's census as being in the Powamuy, the second "order" in the Katsina/Powamuy society, were given a score. Although Taw, Al, and Kwan were also tribal initiation societies, a score was given because they were "more powerful" and fewer men joined them. Thus, a score of 0 societies joined does not imply that the individual was either totally inactive or barred from the ceremonial life, although some individuals may have been inactive or almost so.

CHAPTER 5

1. Except where otherwise noted, this section is based on Spicer (1962:187–98) and Montgomery, Smith, and Brew (1949).

2. The account presented here is drawn from Titiev (1944:69–95) and Whiteley (1988:71–120).

CHAPTER 6

1. It is not clear whether Titiev is counting the total population in 1906 or whether he is including those who are included in his census but who were deceased by 1906. There were 858 individuals counted in the 1900 census living in Orayvi and Munqapi. If Titiev counted everyone over 16 years in 1906, as well as some of those already dead, he would have come up with something over 600 people.

2. Whiteley (1988:203–10, 280) believes that the Hostile faction generally, and those who later went to Paaqavi especially, were of equal rank to the Friendlies. I think he reaches this conclusion because he uses a different definition of pavansinom, one that sees individuals attaining the rank by their own efforts in the ceremonial sphere, or even by becoming a healer. His list of pavansinom at Paaqavi includes people who had died prior to the split (i.e., Masangöntiwa), who had attained office after the split or when the rival Soyal society was established, or who were merely initiated into the Kwan society (Kuwannömtiwa, for example).

3. See an account from Second Mesa told to Voth (1905:10–15).

4. Titiev's notes say that Qötsventiwa was "ex Al Chief." It is not clear whether he resigned his post before the split when the position went to his nephews or whether they had already died when he took over the position and Titiev is referring to the 1930s.

5. Tuuvi (Tuba) may have come originally from Walpi, although Titiev does not record this. The name Tuuvi means "outcast" in Hopi, and rather than being an ally of Loololma as reported by Whiteley (1988:87), he was considered an apostate due to his conversion to Mormonism in the early 1870s. He was, however, a Friendly, as was his brother-in-law. Tuuvi was, according to Titiev, either a Piikyas or a Butterfly clansman who was married to an Eagle woman, Katsinmana.

6. Four Hopi men are named, but Tuuvi is not one of them. He was probably dead by this time. In 1892, there were 20 to 30 Mormon families in Tuba City and Munqapi.

7. Titiev's census notes only that these people were in Munqapi before 1906. As the census was taken in June it is possible that many, if not most, were summer residents only.

8. The Navajo population was between 11,000 and 12,000 in 1865, and between 15,000 and 16,000 in 1890 (Johnston 1966:127–39).

9. Third Mesa women 33+ years were younger on average than those of the other mesas and, in consequence, may have had less chance to lose children. To control for this, only women 33 to 37 years of age were considered. The mean ages did not differ among mesas within this cohort, but Third Mesa women still had significantly better survival rates: 58.3 percent for Third Mesa, between 41 and 42 percent for the other mesas ($p < .01$).

CHAPTER 7
1. For a full discussion of Hopi "shamanism," see Levy (in press)

2. Also mentioned in Titiev's notes was a young man said to have been trained as a poswimkya who had gone insane and died. This was Tuvehongiwma, of Greasewood clan, who was a Hostile and practiced as a shaman but may not have been in the society, which had disbanded by that time.

3. Cushing felt this final section reflected early Mormon teaching.

4. Because his was the first name mentioned, Whiteley (1988:320n7) believes Kui-ian-ai-ni-wa may be another name for Tala'yma (Spider clan), who was chief of Momtsit. The reason for this assumption is not given; it is certain, however, that this man did not give Cushing the creation myth described here, which is clearly a Kookop production. Another unlikely possibility is that "Kui-ian-ai-ni-wa" was Kuwanhoyniwa, of Butterfly (Poovol) clan, who was in his late twenties at this time. In addition to Patupha, the other positively identified

members of the Hostile group who met Cushing were "Kuh-ni-a, the Coznino" (Tuvewuhiwma of Spider clan); "He-vi-ma" (Heevi'ima, Kookop clan); and "Mui-shon-ai-ti-wa" (Masongöntiwa, Snake clan).

5. Among those not previously arrested was Aqawsi, a Navajo Tuuvi had adopted when a boy, who may have joined the Hostiles temporarily after marrying a Hostile woman of Piikyas clan. By the time of the split he had remarried and was living once more in Munqapi. There are also a number of men whose clans were incorrectly identified by Whiteley (1988:87)—probably because the information was obtained from contemporary informants—as Badger, when they were really Gray or Navajo Badgers (Piphongva, Talasyawma, Tawaletstiwa); as Patki but really Piikyas (Sikyaheptiwa); as Desert Fox but really Water Coyote (Qötsyawma); as Parrot but one of the Crows calling themselves Parrots (Polingyawma). These were all men from low-status clans. Only Qötsventiwa (Bow) stands out as high ranking and an important office holder.

6. According to Hopi tradition, Orayvi was founded after two brothers of Bear clan argued and one, Matsito, left Songoopavi and founded Orayvi. Before this time Songoopavi must surely have farmed the floodplain on Orayvi Wash. Over time, the Orayvis expropriated this land and the Second Mesa villages were limited to farming along tributary streams. Orayvi tradition claims that whichever village ultimately has the largest population will triumph over the other. When the myths are told, Second Mesa tellers emphasize Matsito's blame for all the troubles, while those from Third Mesa lay the blame on the chief of Songoopavi.

7. Note that in the creation by Huru'ingwuuti, Spider Grandmother lives in the south, while in this myth she goes north. Similarly, the Mormons are told the Pahaana will come from the west, while the Americans are told he will come from the east.

8. Although Kookop has been translated as "fire brand" or stick, it seems to refer to a small bird with a grayish black mark under its chin resembling ashes; hence its association with fire and Maasaw.

9. A year after this myth was recorded, Wallis (1936:2–17) recorded a version told by the son of the Second Mesa Hostile leader who supported Yukiwma. In this version, Spider Grandmother is the wife of Maasaw who, with the Twin War Gods, helps the people to escape the underworld and also makes the present world habitable. Only witches will cause Hopis to be baptized, and this will be because the White man did not cut off the heads as he, as Older Brother, was supposed to do.

10. Kuwannömtiwa (Sand clan) was married to Lomahongiwma's niece and took over the leadership of Lomahongiwma's group after their return to Orayvi from Hotvela.

11. This account is included in Titiev's census account of households 549–551 headed by Honmana, Loololma's oldest sister. It seems unlikely, however, that Kuwannömtiwa was supposed to become a Christian.

12. In this book, Titiev uses pseudonyms for all but a very few individuals.

13. It is doubtful that a tradition of women Village chiefs can be inferred from the installation of a woman "chief" in Munqapi. When Loololma sent people to Munqapi to defend his claim to the land there, Nasilewnöm, a woman of Piikyas clan, assumed the position of chief. She was never referred to as kik-mongwi but as mö'wi and was only a secular leader, as Munqapi had no clan houses and remained within the ritual system of Orayvi rather than developing its own cycle (Nagata 1970:37–39).

14. This happened sometime in 1966. During that year, a pawnshop in Flag-staff, Arizona, offered a Mexican parrot figurine (made of ceramic covered with inlaid abalone shell) for sale. The Lansas heard about this after I had bought it and wanted to obtain it for themselves to show they owned the Parrot clan fetish and so legitimatize Mina Lansa's claim. More recently, Stanley Paanimp-tiwa returned to Winslow, Arizona, and announced that he was the true leader of Orayvi. Most Orayvis, however, do not accept this claim.

CHAPTER 8

1. It is important to emphasize, however, that upward mobility of clans and even of individuals was not all that frequent. If clans were in a constant state of transforming themselves, and individuals—as in the case of the Crows who called themselves Parrots—were free to change their identity and status at will, none of the significant differences found among clans and lineages in respect of fertility, child survival, longevity, or political affiliation would have had time to develop. Nor should the fact that clans are known to have assumed the identity and responsibilities of a clan that was dying out be taken as justifica-tion for rejecting the definition of the clan as a group of consanguineal kin with descent from an unknown common ancestress. While it is certainly true that true genealogical descent is a social fiction, Hopi society functioned on the principle of common descent. Kin terms were extended to all members of one's own clan as well as to those of one's father's clan and, as the system originated in the myth time immediately after the emergence, in Hopi theory the clan was eternal.

2. As far as I can determine, a cyclical theory of history is not found among the other Pueblos. On the other hand, Hopi concepts are remarkably like those of the Maya. According to the Mayan prophecies, in katun 8 Ahau the Itza capital would fall and be abandoned. Prior to this time the Yucatec Maya had rejected Spanish overtures, claiming the time had not yet come. By 1696, the Spaniards were informed that the time of the prophecy had arrived and the

conquest of the Yucatan was completed. As with the Hopi and the Pahaana, however, one faction disputed the need to capitulate and mounted armed resistance, while another faction was resigned to its fate (Farriss 1987:584–85). The Pahaana prophecy also has an Aztec parallel: the Aztec ruler, Moctezuma, believed that Cortés was the god Quetzalcoatl who, according to prophecy, would return to reclaim his kingdom. The degree to which Aztec, Maya, or Hopi concepts contributed to their conquest and decline, however, is moot. Jones (1982) has shown that the Itza kingdom was already on the defensive, surrounded by a growing number of Spanish settlements and cut off from its wealth in the cacao trade. It seems doubtful that Hopi history would have been very different whether or not the Anglo-Americans were the true Pahaana.

References

Aberle, David F.
   1967   "The Psychosocial Analysis of a Hopi Life History." In *Personalities and Cultures*, Robert Hunt, ed., pp. 79–138. New York: Natural History Press.
   1980   "Navajo Exogamic Rules and Preferred Marriages." In *The Versatility of Kinship: Essays Presented to Harry W. Basehart*, L. S. Cordell and S. Beckerman, eds., pp. 105–43. New York: Academic Press.
Adams, Eleanor B.
   1963   "Fray Silvestre and The Obstinate Hopi." *New Mexico Historical Review* 28: 97–138.
Adams, Eleanor B., and Fray Angelico Chavez
   1956   *The Missions of New Mexico, 1776*. Albuquerque: University of New Mexico Press.
Arnon, Nancy S., and W. W. Hill
   1979   "Santa Clara Pueblo." In *Handbook of North American Indians*. Vol. 9, *Southwest*, Alfonso Ortiz, ed., pp. 296–307. Washington, D.C.: Smithsonian Institution.
Bandelier, Adolf F.
   1892   *Final Report of Investigations among the Indians of the Southwestern United States, Carried on Mainly in the Years from 1880 to 1885*. Cambridge, Massachusetts: John Wilson and Son, University Press.
Beaglehole, Ernest, and Pearl Beaglehole
   1935   "Hopi of the Second Mesa." *American Anthropologist* 44:1–65.
Beaglehole, Pearl
   1935   "Census Data from Two Hopi Villages." *American Anthropologist* 37:41–54.
Bell, Colin, and Howard Newby
   1972   *Community Studies: An Introduction to the Sociology of the Local Community*. New York: Praeger.

Bellah, Robert N.

1952   *Apache Kinship Systems*. Cambridge: Harvard University Press.

Benedict, Ruth

1934   *Patterns of Culture*. Boston: Houghton Mifflin.

Bennett, John W.

1946   "The Interpretation of Pueblo Culture: A Question of Values." *Southwestern Journal of Anthropology* 2:361–74.

Bradfield, Maitland

1971   *The Changing Pattern of Hopi Agriculture*. London: Royal Anthropological Institute of Great Britain and Ireland, Occasional Paper 30.

Brandt, Richard B.

1954   *Hopi Ethics: A Theoretical Analysis*. Chicago: University of Chicago Press.

Brew, John O.

1979   "Hopi Prehistory and History to 1850." In *Handbook of North American Indians*. Vol. 9, *Southwest*, Alfonso Ortiz, ed., pp. 514–23. Washington, D.C.: Smithsonian Institution.

Bunzel, Ruth

1932   "Introduction to Zuni Ceremonialism." U.S. Bureau of American Ethnology *Annual Report* 47:467–544.

Cameron, Catherine M.

1990   "Architectural Change at a Southwestern Pueblo." Ph.D. dissertation, Department of Anthropology, University of Arizona, Tucson.

Carneiro, Robert L.

1987   "Village Splitting as a Function of Population Size." In *Themes in Ethnology and Culture History: Essays in Honor of David F. Aberle*, Leland Donald, ed., pp. 94–124. Meerut, India: Archana Publications for the Folklore Institute.

Cleland, Robert Glass, and Juanita Brooks, eds.

1955   *A Mormon Chronicle: The Diaries of John D. Lee, 1848–1876*. San Marino, California: The Huntington Library.

Clemmer, Richard O.

1978   *Continuities of Hopi Culture Change*. Ramona, California: Acoma Books.

Connelly, John C.

1979   "Hopi Social Organization." In *Handbook of North American Indians*. Vol. 9, *Southwest*, Alfonso Ortiz, ed., pp. 539–53. Washington, D.C.: Smithsonian Institution.

Coues, Elliott

1900   *On the Trail of a Spanish Pioneer*. New York: Harper.

Courlander, Harold

1971   *The Fourth World of the Hopis*. New York: Crown Publishers.

1982   *Hopi Voices: Recollections, Traditions, and Narratives of the Hopi Indians*. Albuquerque: University of New Mexico Press.

Crane, Leo

1925   *Indians of the Enchanted Desert*. Boston: Little Brown.

Cushing, Frank Hamilton

1883   "Zuni Fetishes." U.S. Bureau of American Ethnology *Annual Report* 2:9–43.

1922   "Oraibi in 1883." In "Contributions to Hopi History," *American Anthropologist* 24:253–68.

1923   "Origin Myth from Oraibi." *Journal of American Folklore* 36:163–70.

Donaldson, Thomas
   1893   *Moqui Pueblo Indians of Arizona and Pueblo Indians of New Mexico: Extra Census
           Bulletin*. Washington D.C.: U.S. Census Printing Office.

Dorsey, George A., and Henry R. Voth
   1901   "The Oraibi Soyal Ceremony." *Field Columbian Museum Publication* 55, Anthro-
           pological Series 3(1):1–59.

Dozier, Edward P.
   1966   "Factionalism at Santa Clara Pueblo." *Ethnology* 5:172–85.
   1970   *The Pueblo Indians of North America*. New York: Holt, Rinehart, and Winston.

Dyen, Isidore, and David F. Aberle
   1974   *Lexical Reconstruction: The Case of the Proto-Athabascan Kinship System*. London:
           Cambridge University Press.

Edelman, Sandra A.
   1979   "San Ildefonso Pueblo." In *Handbook of North American Indians*. Vol. 9, *South-
           west*, Alfonso Ortiz, ed., pp. 308–16. Washington, D.C.: Smithsonian In-
           stitution.

Eggan, Dorothy
   1943   "The General Problem of Hopi Adjustment." *American Anthropologist* 45:357–
           73.

Eggan, Fred
   1949   "The Hopi and the Lineage Principle." In *Social Structure: Studies Presented to
           A. R. Radcliffe-Brown*, Myer Fortes, ed., pp. 121–44. New York: Russell and
           Russell.
   1950   *Social Organization of the Western Pueblos*. Chicago: University of Chicago
           Press.
   1966   *The American Indian: Perspectives for the Study of Social Change*. Chicago: Aldine
           Publishing Co.
   1967   "From History to Myth: A Hopi Example." In *Studies in Southwestern Ethno-
           linguistics*, Dell Hymes and William E. Bittle, eds., pp. 33–53. The Hague:
           Mouton & Company.
   1975   "Alliance and Descent in a Western Pueblo Society." In *Essays in Social Anthro-
           pology and Ethnology*, pp. 275–85. Chicago: Department of Anthropology,
           University of Chicago. Originally published in *Process and Patterns in Cul-
           ture*, Robert A. Manners, ed., pp. 175–84. Chicago: Aldine Publishing Co.,
           1964.
   1980   "Shoshone Kinship Structures and Their Significance for Anthropological
           Theory." *Journal of the Steward Anthropological Society* 11:165–93.

Ellis, Florence Hawley
   1979   "Laguna Pueblo." In *Handbook of North American Indians*. Vol. 9, *Southwest*,
           Alfonso Ortiz, ed., pp. 438–49. Washington, D.C.: Smithsonian Institution.

Engels, Friedrich
   1942   *The Origin of the Family, Private Property and the State in the Light of the Researches
           of Lewis H. Morgan*. New York: International Publishers.

Faris, James C.
   1990   *The Nightway: A History of Documentation of a Navajo Ceremonial*. Albuquerque:
           University of New Mexico Press.

Farriss, Nancy M.
  1987 "Remembering the Future, Anticipating the Past: History, Time, and Cosmology among the Maya of Yucatan." *Comparative Studies in Society and History* 29:566–93.
Fenton, William N.
  1957 "Factionalism at Taos Pueblo, New Mexico." *Anthropological Papers* 56, *Bureau of American Ethnology Bulletin* 164:277–344.
Fewkes, J. Walter
  1922 "Oraibi in 1890." In "Contributions to Hopi History," *American Anthropologist* 24:253–99.
Forbes, Jack D.
  1966 "The Early Western Apache, 1300–1700." *Journal of the West* 5:336–54.
Forde, C. Daryll
  1931 "Hopi Agriculture and Land Ownership." *Journal of the Royal Anthropological Institute* 41:357–405.
French, David H.
  1948 *Factionalism in Isleta*. Monographs of the American Ethnological Society 14.
Fried, Morton H.
  1960 "On the Evolution of Social Stratification and the State." In *Culture in History*, Stanley Diamond, ed., pp. 713–31. New York: Columbia University Press.
Frigout, Arlette
  1979 "Hopi Ceremonial Organization." In *Handbook of North American Indians*. Vol. 9, *Southwest*, Alfonso Ortiz, ed., pp. 564–76. Washington, D.C.: Smithsonian Institution.
Goldfrank, Esther
  1945 "Socialization, Personality, and the Structure of Pueblo Society." *American Anthropologist* 47:516–39.
  1948 "The Impact of Situation and Personality on Four Hopi Emergence Myths." *Southwestern Journal of Anthropology* 4:241–62.
Goodwin, Grenville
  1969 *The Social Organization of the Western Apache*. 1st ed. 1942. Tucson: University of Arizona Press.
Gough, Kathleen
  1961 "Variation in Matrilineal Systems." In *Matrilineal Kinship*, D. M. Schneider and K. Gough, eds., pp. 445–652. Berkeley: University of California Press.
Grant, Campbell
  1978 *Canyon de Chelly: Its People and Rock Art*. Tucson: University of Arizona Press.
Griffith, James S.
  1983 "Kachinas and Masking." In *Handbook of North American Indians*. Vol. 10, *Southwest*, Alfonso Ortiz, ed., pp. 764–77. Washington, D.C.: Smithsonian Institution.
Gumerman, George G., and Jeffrey S. Dean
  1989 "Prehistoric Cooperation and Competition in the Western Anasazi Area." In *Dynamics of Southwest Prehistory*, Linda S. Cordell and George G. Gumerman, eds., pp. 99–148. Washington, D.C.: Smithsonian Institution Press. A School of American Research Advanced Seminar Book.

Haas, Jonathan, and Winifred Creamer

1985 "Warfare and Tribalization in the Prehistoric Southwest: Report on the First Season's Work, 1984." Report submitted to the Harry Frank Guggenheim Foundation, New York. Santa Fe, New Mexico: School of American Research.

Hack, John T.

1942 *The Changing Physical Environment of the Hopi Indians of Arizona.* Papers of the Peabody Museum of Archaeology and Ethnology, vol. 35, no. 1. Awatovi Expedition Report 1. Cambridge: Harvard University.

Hacker, Andrew, ed.

1983 *U/S: A Statistical Portrait of the American People.* New York: The Viking Press.

Hackett, Charles Wilson

1937 *Historical Documents Relating to New Mexico, Nueva Vizcaya, and Approaches Thereto, to 1773.* Vol. 3. Washington, D.C.: Carnegie Institution.

Hammond, George, and Agapito Rey

1966 *The Rediscovery of New Mexico, 1580–1594.* Albuquerque: University of New Mexico Press.

Hegmon, Michelle

1989 "Risk Reduction and Variation in Agricultural Economies: A Computer Simulation of Hopi Agriculture. *Research in Economic Anthropology* 11:89–121.

Heider, Karl G.

1988 "The Rashomon Effect: When Ethnographers Disagree." *American Anthropologist* 90:73–81.

Henderson, Eric B., and Jerrold E. Levy

1975 "Survey of Navajo Community Studies." *Lake Powell Research Project Bulletin* 6. Los Angeles: Institute of Physics and Geophysics, University of California.

Hieb, Louis A.

1979 "Hopi World View." In *Handbook of North American Indians.* Vol. 9, *Southwest*, Alfonso Ortiz, ed., pp. 577–80. Washington, D.C.: Smithsonian Institution.

Johansson, S. Ryan, and S. H. Preston

1978 "Tribal Demography: The Hopi and Navaho Populations as Seen Through Manuscripts from the 1900 U.S. Census." *Social Science History* 3:1–33.

Johnston, Denis Foster

1966 *An Analysis of Sources of Information on the Population of the Navajo.* Bureau of American Ethnology Bulletin 197. Washington, D.C.: U.S. Government Printing Office.

Jones, Grant D.

1982 "Agriculture and Trade in the Colonial Period Southern Maya Lowlands." In *Maya Subsistence: Studies in Memory of Dennis E. Puleston*, Kent V. Flannery, ed., pp. 275–93. New York: Academic Press.

Jorgensen, Joseph G.

1980 *Western Indians: Comparative Environments, Languages, and Cultures of 172 Western American Indian Tribes.* San Francisco: W. H. Freeman & Co.

1987 "Political Society in Aboriginal Western North America." In *Themes in Ethnology and Culture History: Essays in Honor of David F. Aberle*, Leland Donald, ed., pp. 175–226. Meerut, India: Archana Publications for the Folklore Institute.

Kennard, Edward A.

    n.d.   "Genealogies of the Third Mesa Villages." Ms., Laboratory of Anthropology, Santa Fe.

    1972   "Metaphor and Magic: Key Concepts in Hopi Culture and Their Linguistic Forms." In *Studies in Linguistics in Honor of George L. Trager*, M. Estellie Smith, ed., pp. 468–73. The Hague: Mouton.

Kent, Kate Peck

    1983   *Pueblo Indian Textiles: A Living Tradition*. Santa Fe: School of American Research Press.

Kroeber, Alfred L.

    1917   *Zuni Kin and Clan*. American Museum of Natural History, Anthropological Papers, vol. 18, pt. 2.

Lange, Charles H.

    1968   *Cochiti: A New Mexico Pueblo Past and Present*. 1st ed. 1959. Carbondale: Southern Illinois University Press.

Leupp, Francis E.

    1906   *Annual Report of the Commissioner of Indian Affairs*. Washington, D.C.: U.S. Government Printing Office.

Lewton, Frederick L.

    1913   "The Cotton of the Hopi Indians." *Smithsonian Miscellaneous Collections* 60, no. 6:1–15.

Levy, Jerrold E.

    n.d.   "Hopi Shamanism: A Reappraisal." In *Essays in Honor of Fred Eggan*, A. Ortiz and R. de Mallie, eds. Norman: University of Oklahoma Press.

Levy, Jerrold E., and Stephen J. Kunitz

    1974   *Indian Drinking: Navajo Practices and Anglo-American Theories*. New York: John Wiley and Sons.

    1987   "A Suicide Prevention Program for Hopi Youth." *Social Science and Medicine* 25:931–40.

Levy, Jerrold E., Eric B. Henderson, and Tracy J. Andrews

    1989   "The Effects of Regional Variation and Temporal Change on Matrilineal Elements of Navajo Social Organization." *Journal of Anthropological Research* 45: 351–77.

Levy, Jerrold E., Stephen J. Kunitz, and Eric B. Henderson

    1987   "Hopi Deviance in Historical and Epidemiological Perspective." In *Themes in Ethnology and Culture History: Essays in Honor of David F. Aberle*, Leland Donald, ed., pp. 355–96. Meerut, India: Archana Publications for the Folklore Institute.

Little, James A.

    1909   *Jacob Hamblin: A Personal Narrative*. 1st ed. 1882. Salt Lake City: Deseret News.

Lowie, Robert H.

    1929   "Notes on Hopi Clans." The American Museum of Natural History, *Anthropological Papers* 30:303–60.

Malinowski, Bronislaw

    1926   *Myth in Primitive Psychology*. New York: W. W. Norton.

Martin, Debra L.

    1990   "Patterns of Health and Disease: Stress Profiles for the Prehistoric Southwest." Paper prepared for the advanced seminar, "The Organization and Evolution of Prehistoric Southwestern Society." School of American Research, Santa Fe, New Mexico, September 25–29, 1989.

McClintock, James H.
1921 *Mormon Settlement in Arizona: A Record of Peaceful Conquest of the Desert.* Phoenix, Arizona.

McIntire, Elliot G.
1970 "Hopi Indian Population Change." Paper presented at the 14th annual meeting of the Arizona Academy of Science. Phoenix, Arizona, April 18, 1970.

Mindeleff, Cosmos
1900 "Localization of Tusayan Clans." *Nineteenth Annual Report of the Bureau of American Ethnology, for the Years 1897–1898*, pp. 635–53. Washington, D.C.: U.S. Government Printing Office.

Mindeleff, Victor
1891 "A Study of Pueblo Architecture: Tusayan and Cibola." *Eighth Annual Report of the Bureau of American Ethnology, for the Years 1886–1887*, pp. 3–228. Washington, D.C.: U.S. Government Printing Office.

Montgomery, Ross G., Watson Smith, and John O. Brew
1949 *Franciscan Awatovi: The Excavation and Conjectural Reconstruction of a 17th Century Spanish Mission Establishment at a Hopi Indian Town in Northeastern Arizona.* Papers of the Peabody Museum of Archaeology and Ethnology, vol. 36. Cambridge: Harvard University.

Murdock, George Peter
1965 *Social Structure.* 1st ed. 1949. New York: Free Press.

Nagata, Shuichi
1970 *Modern Transformations of Moenkopi Pueblo.* Urbana: University of Illinois Press.
1978 "Dan Kochongva's Message: Myth, Ideology and Political Action among the Contemporary Hopi." In *The Yearbook of Symbolic Anthropology.* Vol. 1, Eric Schwimmer, ed., pp. 73–87. London: C. Hurst and Company.

New Mexico State Record Center Archives
1801 *Extracto de los novedads ocuridas en la Provincia del Nuevo Mexico desde 1º de Abril hasta 12 de Junio de 1801.* Spanish Archives no. 1548. Santa Fe.

Nisbet, Robert A.
1969 *Social Change and History: Aspects of the Western Theory of Development.* London: Oxford University Press.

Parsons, Elsie Clews
1922 "Oraibi in 1920." In "Contributions to Hopi History," *American Anthropologist* 24:253–99.
1925 *A Pueblo Indian Journal.* American Anthropological Association Memoir 32.
1929 *The Social Organization of the Tewa of New Mexico.* American Anthropological Association Memoir 36.
1933 *Hopi and Zuni Ceremonialism.* American Anthropological Association Memoir 39.
1939 *Pueblo Indian Religion.* Chicago: University of Chicago Press.

Plog, Fred, George J. Gumerman, Robert C. Euler, Jeffrey S. Dean, Richard H. Hevly, and Thor N. V. Karlstrom
1988 "Anasazi Adaptive Strategies: The Model, Predictions, and Results." In *The Anasazi in a Changing Environment*, George J. Gumerman, ed., pp. 230–76.

Cambridge: Cambridge University Press. A School of American Research Advanced Seminar Book.

Powell, Walter Clement
1948– "W. C. Powell's Account of the Hopi Towns." *Utah Historical Quarterly* 16 and
49   17:479–90.

Redfield, Robert
1955   *The Little Community: Viewpoints for the Study of a Human Whole.* Chicago: University of Chicago Press.

Sekaquaptewa, Helen
1969   *Me and Mine: The Life Story of Helen Sekaquaptewa.* As told to Louise Udall. Tucson: University of Arizona Press.

Siegel, Bernard J.
1955   "High Anxiety Levels and Cultural Integration: Notes on a Psycho-Cultural Hypothesis." *Social Forces* 34:42–48.

Simmons, Marc
1979   "History of the Pueblos Since 1821." In *Handbook of North American Indians.* Vol. 9, *Southwest,* Alfonso Ortiz, ed., pp. 206–23. Washington, D.C.: Smithsonian Institution.

Spicer, Edward H.
1962   *Cycles of Conquest: The Impact of Spain, Mexico, and the United States on the Indians of the Southwest, 1533–1960.* Tucson: University of Arizona Press.

Steen, Charlie R.
1966   *Tse Ta'a: Excavations at Tse Ta'a, Canyon de Chelly National Monument, Arizona.* National Park Service Research Series 9. Washington, D.C.

Stephen, Alexander M.
1929   "Hopi Tales." *Journal of American Folklore* 42:1–62.
1969   *Hopi Journal of Alexander M. Stephen.* 1st. ed. 1936. Elsie Clews Parsons, ed. 2 vols. New York: AMS Press.

Steward, Julian H.
1955   *Theory of Culture Change: The Methodology of Multilinear Evolution.* Urbana: University of Illinois Press.

Talayesva, Don C.
1942   *Sun Chief: The Autobiography of a Hopi Indian.* Leo W. Simmons, ed. New Haven: Yale University Press.

Tambiah, S. J.
1965   "Kinship Fact and Fiction in Relation to the Kandyan Sinhalese." *Journal of the Royal Anthropological Institute* 95:131–73.

Thomas, Alfred Barnaby
1932   *Forgotten Frontiers: A Study of the Spanish Indian Policy of Don Juan Bautista de Anza, Governor of New Mexico, 1777–1780.* Norman: University of Oklahoma Press.

Thompson, Laura
1945   "Logico-Aesthetic Integration in Hopi Culture." *American Anthropologist* 47: 540–53.
1950   *Culture in Crisis: A Study of the Hopi Indians.* New York: Harper and Brothers.

Thompson, Laura, and Alice Joseph
1947   *The Hopi Way.* Chicago: University of Chicago Press. (Reprint of 1944 ed.)

Thornthwaite, C. Warren, C. F. Stewart Sharpe, and Earl F. Dosch
1942 "Climate and Accelerated Erosion in the Arid and Semi-arid Southwest, with Special Reference to the Polacca Wash Drainage Basin, Arizona." *U.S. Dept. of Agriculture, Technical Bulletin* 808. Washington D.C.

Titiev, Mischa
1938 "The Problem of Cross-Cousin Marriage among the Hopi." *American Anthropologist* 40:105–11.
1942 "Notes on Hopi Witchcraft." *Michigan Academy of Science, Arts, and Letters, Papers* 28:549–57. (Published 1943.)
1944 *Old Oraibi: A Study of the Hopi Indians of Third Mesa*. Papers of the Peabody Museum of American Archaeology and Ethnology, vol. 2, no. 1. Cambridge: Harvard University.
1946 "Review of 'The Hopi Way'." *American Anthropologist* 48:430–32.
1972 *The Hopi Indians of Old Oraibi: Change and Continuity*. Ann Arbor: University of Michigan Press.
n.d. "Census Notes from Old Oraibi." Ms., Peabody Museum of Archaeology and Ethnology. Cambridge: Harvard University.

Tyler, Hamilton A.
1964 *Pueblo Gods and Myths*. Norman: University of Oklahoma Press.

U.S. Census of Population
1900 "Population Census Schedules: Moqui Indian Reservation." National Archives of the United States. Microfilm Roll T623, Reel 48.

Underhill, Ruth M.
1948 *Ceremonial Patterns in the Greater Southwest*. American Ethnological Society Monograph 13:1–62.

Vaillant, George C.
1962 *Aztecs of Mexico: Origin, Rise and Fall of the Aztec Nation*. 2nd rev. ed. New York: Penguin Books.

Vidich, Arthur J., and Joseph Bensman
1958 *Small Town in Mass Society: Class, Power, and Religion in a Rural Community*. Princeton: Princeton University Press.

Vincent, Joan
1978 "Political Anthropology: Manipulative Strategies." *Annual Review of Anthropology* 7:175–94.

Voth, Henry R.
1901 "The Oraibi Powamu Ceremony." *Field Columbian Museum Publication* 55, *Anthropological Series* 3(2):64–158.
1905 *The Traditions of the Hopi*. Chicago: Field Columbian Museum.

Wallis, Wilson Dallam
1936 "Folk Tales from Sumopovi, Second Mesa." *Journal of American Folklore* 49:1–68.

Welton, H. S.
1888 Welton to Commissioner of Indian Affairs. Letter. June 17, 1888. National Archives, Record Group 75, Office of Indian Affairs, Land Records, File 15959/1888.

West, James
1945 *Plainville, U.S.A.* New York: Columbia University Press.

Whiteley, Peter M.

    1985   "Unpacking Hopi 'Clans': Another Vintage Model Out of Africa?" *Journal of Anthropological Research* 41:359–74.

    1986   "Unpacking Hopi 'Clans' II: Further Questions About Hopi Descent Groups." *Journal of Anthropological Research* 42:69–79.

    1988   *Deliberate Acts: Changing Hopi Culture Through the Oraibi Split*. Tucson: University of Arizona Press.

Wright, Gary A.

    1978   "The Shoshone Migration Problem." *Plains Anthropologist* 23:113–37.

Yava, Albert

    1978   *Big Falling Snow: A Tewa-Hopi Indian's Life and Times and the History and Traditions of His People*. Harold Courlander, ed. and annot. New York: Crown Publishers.

Index